Aging in America

By the author of

No Language But a Cry
Your Nonlearning Child

Aging in America

BERT KRUGER SMITH

BEACON PRESS   BOSTON

Copyright © 1973 by Bert Kruger Smith

Beacon Press books are published under the auspices
of the Unitarian Universalist Association

First published as a Beacon Paperback in 1974

Published simultaneously in Canada by Saunders of Toronto, Ltd.

All rights reserved

Printed in the United States of America

9 8 7 6 5 4 3

Library of Congress Cataloging in Publication Data

Smith, Bert (Kruger) 1915–
   Aging in America.
   Includes bibliographical references.
   1. Aged—United States. 2. Old age. I. Title.
[DNLM: 1. Aging. 2. Geriatrics—U.S. WT 104
S643a 1973]
HQ1064.U5S58   301.43′5′0973   72–6232
ISBN 0–8070–2768–5
ISBN 0–8070–2769–3 (pbk.)

This book is dedicated, with love, to each member of my wonderful family

Contents

Acknowledgments

Acknowledgments are boxes which hold only portions of their material. Many people help with the composition of a book, and in a number of ways. Some give tangible aid in reading, criticizing, and making suggestions or in typing, proofing, or doing reference work. Others assist by their ideas and discussions of various aspects of the manuscript. Still others aid by personal support and concern. There are those who by example and by endurance demonstrate some of the ideas set forth. Finally, there are the thinkers, writers, poets who have put down principles, philosophies, and expressions which have served to undergird many of the ideas presented in the book. To all of them go my thanks.

As always, my immediate family members have been both encouraging and supportive in numerous ways. To Sid, Shel, Randy, and Mother—and to Linda, Stacy, Russell, and Jon goes my loving appreciation.

Dr. Wayne H. Holtzman, President of the Hogg Foundation, merits special thanks for encouraging me to write the book and for serving as critical reader of it. Drs. Robert L. Sutherland and Bernice Milburn Moore of the Hogg Foundation supplied helpful ideas and editorial aid. Dr. Ira Iscoe performed a double role, as idea stimulator and as critical reader.

Arnold C. Tovell, editor-in-chief of Beacon Press, extended his interest, support, and assistance beyond the usual editorial function. His thoughtful suggestions were growth producing. Lois Randall, as copy editor, was a concerned partner in the endeavor.

Others on the Hogg Foundation staff deserve individual mention, including Cindy Boyd, for her special and enduring help, along with Ruby Baker, Charlene Booth, Jilda Bottoni, Dorothe Bozza, and Reymundo Rodriguez.

Drs. Hiram Friedsam, Charles Gaitz, Chad Gordon, Herbert Shore, Guy Shuttlesworth, and Richard Sinclair aided in specific ways. Allen Skidmore, Lucinda Pardo, Carter Clopton, and members of the Governor's Committee on Aging merit regard for their assistance. Finally, Dr. Bertram S. Brown, who wrote the Introduction, was greatly helpful.

Introduction

BERTRAM S. BROWN, M.D.

Director, National Institute of Mental Health

The riddle that the Sphinx poses to Oedipus is: "What animal walks on four feet in the morning, two feet at noon, and three feet in the evening?" As we remember, the answer is Man—crawling in the morning, walking erect at noontime, and walking with the assistance of a cane in old age. For too long we have ignored the three-footed and four-footed parts of humanity.

This book concerns the three-legged human that all of us will become or already have become. It tells our story in a clear and moving way. I recommend this book for professionals, the aged, and all concerned individuals. In America approximately one-tenth of our population are now over the age of sixty-five. In the first chapter we are told who the aged are: "They are people like all of us. They are educated and they are simple. They are wealthy and they are on welfare. They are part of life and they are isolated. They are well and they are desperately ill. They are productive and they are dependent. They are warm and they are mean." The book portrays all these people well.

Old age need not be a time of despair, isolation, and hopelessness. The book moves from a description of the aged to positive steps which can and must be taken by them and for them. As people live differently, so do they age differently. Individual planning for aging has to weigh these differences. Throughout the book many well-drawn sketches of the elderly show not only difficulties of this period but also ways that mental health can be enjoyed. The book discusses both individual planning and collective planning. Programs for the elderly are detailed with examples of how such programs can be instituted. The White House Conference for the Aging and some of its recommendations are reviewed. Our individual responsibility for the present aged and those to come is stressed.

Growing old is an inherent part of the human experience. What Bert Kruger Smith has done so well is to relate to the aging human. The way to actualize the potential for a meaningful and enriched period at the end of one's life is considered in depth. As aging affects us all, this book is relevant for us all.

Aging in America

An Old Woman Speaks

What is it to be a human being? Am I but a reflection cast into the lives of other persons? The schizophrenic child often fears the mirror because he is not sure his likeness will be there. Perhaps the older person withdraws from the picture he knows he reflects in others.

Does a tree falling in the forest make a sound if there are no ears to hear it? Is a person human when he has shrunk into the basic core of self and others have moved away like loose-hanging folds of skin?

What is the sound I make when I am old? Shuffling for sustenance, napping for strength, dressing for no one, waiting for one certain visitor, I am a diminished me. No capital *I*. No self to fling free, a bird sailing skyward. There is only a small *i*, shriveled within the layers of the years.

The evening hours fall suddenly, shutting out the slanting light which livens the corners of my home. The evening hours are a door slammed shut against both friends and laughter.

Somewhere in the early sleepless morning, when daylight still brings flicker of promise, I lie young on my scarcely wrinkled bed and am warmed by the feel of husband-hands caressing me knowingly or of child-fingers on my face or of friend-touch on my hands. But those moments pass. Daytime brings no warmth, and at last I rise because I have always risen and go to prepare myself for a day which stays too shortly and a night which comes too soon.

I am an island, barren, surrounded by the waters of my life, my own shores drouth-pounded, desiccated. Only echoes skim the waters to my island-world—whispers and words, songs and laughter, carried by satellite of memory into my solitude.

Hands lie heavy on my lap—vein-ridged, spotted. Once they were like white birds in graceful flight over keys of a piano, stirring savory pots of food, gentling a crying child. Agile, useful, they were never still. Now they too are done with reaching out. They are folded inward.

Memory teases me, evanescent, transforms me in a breath of time into a bride holding fear and hope inside my white voile wedding dress. I am young and breathless with excitement. . . . No, i am old and breathless with fatigue.

"I know; I know," they say. "There are problems with being old." But they do not know. Everyone has been a child. All can understand through muffled memory how childhood was. But none has been old except those who are that now.

Who can speak for the old? And who speaks to us? Once, when I was very ill, I lay unmoving on a bed. The doctor-voices, nurse-rustles all came to me, barely sounding through the layers of pain which separated us from one another. They talked about me then as if I were not a feeling, hearing human being. They talked above me and around me as they prepared needles and moved limbs. It was as if I had left my body there to be tended.

And now it is the same. No one looks at me—at me, into my eyes, into the core of me. It is "as if" I am like all who have lived too long, a being to be tolerated or bypassed or humored.

Can no one see that within my soul *I* exist? The person who loved and grieved and was? I too have hungered, been tormented by passion, known knife-thrust of pain. Stir the ashes of my being, blow tenderly to bring the flames to light.

Yesterday has fled into the nighttime of the past. The imprint remains, like dew on the fall grasses—the life-smell of sun on a golden rose or of fall grass in the hair of a little boy. The telescope of the mind reverses. What was very close is now remote in the filled closet of memory.

Once I too walked through the hills in the near-rain. The trees were etched clear green, while new-wet brush in the distance seemed filtered like an unfocused picture into vague designs.

So with youth and age. For you who are young, life is close, free-form, clear-colored, significant. For us who are old, the distance of the years turns images into misty shapes, unclear and indistinguishable from one another.

In the daytime, life moves to the cadence of activity. Voices sound down the street, in the house, through the radio. Music plays somewhere. Cars cough; lawnmowers grumble. The teapot whistles.

But at night, the sounds are muffled under a pillow of darkness. The people-noises disappear, and things become animated. A window shade taps on and off in the breeze; a tree whispers against a glass pane. A floor board squeaks and a furnace growls.

The night is still and very lonely.

The autumn sun cannot warm my bones. Yet this day is mine, lying newborn like a shivering duckling in my hands. Can I create of it a memory to note with others in the album of my life? Will I live it, or endure it? I make the choice, knowing that life is not a picture postcard, caught forever at a moment of romantic beauty. Venice with its gondolas and singing boatmen is also Venice with problems of pollution and unemployment. Only memory, or love, or will can pin the butterfly wings of a moment onto the board of time.

To create that moment is to be open, a cup to be filled from the sweet essence of experience. To lie in the heart of life, to feel the pain of a stranger or the joy of a friend, is to be alive—fully alive at any age.

Bring me to soft fire that I may still give warmth to others . . .

The Aging—Who Are They?

Erich Fromm has said, "Birth is only one particular step in a continuum which begins with conception and ends with death. All that is between these two poles is a process of giving birth to one's potentialities, of bringing to life all that is potentially given in the two cells . . . the development of the self is never completed; even under best conditions only part of man's potentialities is realized. Man always dies before he is fully born." [1]

This book concerns itself with the aged. Who are they? What does the word convey? It is said; the label appears; with computer efficiency our minds sort out and place the "aged" into the appropriate slot. Once we have labeled them, we can be comfortable. We need not open the box marked "old" and look inside at the individual forms. Packaged together, they comprise a unit.

Labeling can substitute for thinking or, even more importantly, for feeling. If we place labels on a person, a label like "old" or "black" or "schizophrenic" or "mentally retarded," we can use the stereotype in place of perception.

However, if we want to know the humanness of the persons behind the label, if we want to see the hurt or need, to feel the pain or delight; if we recognize that part of us resides in each of them and part of them in us—then we tear off the labels and begin to see the individuals.

Whom do we mean when we say "aged"?

Do we mean Mrs. Hamilton, living on the hill in the enormous home which her husband bought with his banking money? Her long-time maid and chauffeur grow old with her, but her money buys her medical care and fine foods and personal attention. Does Mrs. Hamilton represent the old?

Or is it Minnie Fuller, in quiet desperation in the rooming-house near the new freeway? She is in genteel aloneness, with no warmth of companionship in the corners of her life. Only her small Social Security payments and an old scrapbook about her early acting attest to the fact that she is alive at all.

Are the aged represented by Stanley Truett who, at 88, still does consulting for an oil company and who lives in dignity in a downtown apartment?

Or does Mike Matthews, only six blocks away, represent the old? He sleeps wherever there is a place, at the Salvation Army or the police station or with an old army friend. Now that he is growing too aged to do any carpentry, he has begun to ask for handouts and to find his warmth inside the frequent bottles of inexpensive wine.

Then there are the Vaughans who, together, continue to participate in many community affairs. They do not attend all of the meetings they once did, but they keep reaching out to other people.

Or Al Sanders, dying of lung disease from his years in the mine, might signify the old. Most of his life has been spent in the dark world beneath his little village, and now he asks his wife to put him near the window where he can feel the sun before he returns to the darkness underground.

Flora Offerman might speak for the elderly. She is very old, her swollen hands curved from years of bathing other peoples' kids and washing other folks' dishes. The members of the church and one of her kids keep her with enough to eat, and former employers come about once a year with some leftover clothes.

Harold Tankersley too is old, but he still hates—hates his infirmity and hates even more all of the people he has always despised—the liberals and the Mexicans, the blacks and the Jews, the professors and executives. Age has not thinned the thick potion of hatred which Harold spills on anyone who stops close by.

Then there is Dolores Martinez. She is in the rocking chair in her two-room house. Such a nice house built by her sons, full of color, paper flowers everywhere. Dolores spends much time on her porch watching the neighbors and their children. Her own children and grandchildren see to it that she is neither lonely nor hungry.

What about Vera Gattis? You will have to go to the state hospital to find her. She sits in the straight chair in the corner of the big recreation room. At least her body in the cotton dress is there. Her mind—well, no one can reach it now or find that core of self which once was Vera Gattis, teacher, mother, woman.

Gus Harvey too is old, nursing-home old. No one comes to see him anymore, and the aides grow weary of changing his wet bed and forcing food through his rigid lips.

There is Gladys Clark, desperately battling illness and senility. She covers pain and forgetfulness with a gentle manner. She works at putting her papers in order while she is alive and can remember.

Or, Norma Garza, migrant worker, still traveling with the truckloads of fruitpickers to the south of Texas every year. She is not fast anymore, but she is old and in need of the little money and of the companionship of others.

Carlos Miguel is Puerto Rican. He never learned to speak English; he never learned a skill which could bring him enough money. And now he is old, quite old, and alone in a house which has been condemned—like him.

The forgetfulness or repetitions of the old may be an annoyance to the young. For the elderly themselves the traits may be filled with a particular kind of terror. The arthritis-bound composer down the block sits in her chair by the front window. A bar comes to her mind, then a phrase, then a line of music, original and sweet. She holds it with joy while she rises from her chair and makes her way to the table where her music pad and pencil lie. But memory is short and movement is slow. By the time her swollen fingers reach the pencil, the tune has played itself out in her mind.

Or, the old man across town, now too feeble to keep his job as school custodian, starts to call his daughter to pick up some groceries for him when she comes home from work. He starts for the telephone but then heads for the kitchen for a cup of tea, the mission forgotten.

Even more frightening is the case of the little woman in the efficiency apartment near the bank building. She tries frantically to hold on to her independence. But she either fails to take her medicine, or she takes it twice. When she cooks, the whole apartment house is in hazard, for she may move to her cot and take a nap without any memory or awareness that eggs are boiling on top of her stove.

Memory is like a long-ago movie screen with characters racing in sight and then out, chasing one another in speeding sequences of flying feet or careening open automobiles. Thoughts come and flee outside the screen of recollection. Events are recalled and removed in almost the same frame. Sometimes happenings of many years ago collide with those of yesterday and become fixed in a single scene without demarcations of time or place.

Memory, fantasy, and time often melt into changing patterns, as varied as those of a child's kaleidoscope. Reality and myth are crumbled together with the pestle of time in the mortar of aging. And for the aged themselves the process is filled with special pain.

This book concerns itself with the aged. Who are they?

They are people like all of us. They are educated and they are simple. They are wealthy and they are on welfare. They are part of life and they are isolated. They are well and they are desperately ill. They are productive and they are dependent. They are warm and they are mean. They give of themselves to others and they withhold themselves totally from the world.

They are human. Many of them fight for that humanness. As they begin to grow forgetful or to suffer from loss of competence, they battle for that quality which says they are alive, they are real, they are remembered, they are cherished. Some are concerned about what constitutes "living," and they beg their physicians to end their physical lives if their minds deteriorate to such an extent that they are unknowing animals instead of feeling human beings.

WHEN IS A PERSON OLD?

The answer may lie within the person asking the question or the one responding. Cicero, speaking of the aged, referred to persons in their sixties and early seventies. But that was in 48 B.C. when life expectancy was much shorter. Aristotle declared that the body is in its prime from thirty to five and thirty, the mind about forty-nine. Plato thought that the age of fifty was the time when a person reached his best peak, having replaced the impatience of his young years with the wisdom of his experience.

When is a person old? Is it when emotionally he sees that the road he is facing is shorter than the one he has walked? Is it the day his teenaged son beats him at golf for the first time? Or does it happen when a woman makes an appointment with a new physician and finds that he resembles her own son? Does it happen on the job? At home? In social life? In bed? Or at all those times and places?

In earlier cultures with shorter life expectancy and larger families, parents bustled through the years trying to feed, clothe, and help their children reach maturity. Their life's task completed, they had a brief span of time to relax from their labors.

But more recently the gift of life, of expectancy of more than three score years and ten and often many more, brings with it longer years of marriage, frequently passing the half-century mark, shorter years of working, and increased time for leisure. Without job definition or expectation, many older people find themselves bewildered, displaced, annoyed, and bypassed. In a work culture they have worked. In a leisure culture they are lost.

Ask the old man in the nursing home. You know the one we mean. He is sitting apart in the slat-bottom rocker. He is not rocking, hardly moving. His white face and whiter hair give a macabre clown's look above the dark suit. There is in his straight mouth no trace of a one-time smile. His eyes are open—but they look at nothing.

Go ahead. Ask him what it is to be old. Let him tell you. You'll have to yell because he can scarcely hear. You may even need to shake his shoulder a bit. He is not used to being talked to. But when you get his attention, state your question. Then wait.

He will answer slowly, so slowly that you wonder if he will speak at all. When he talks, his voice will be like that of a person trying to communicate through the effects of anesthesia. He will shake his head slowly and then lay his hands carefully before him—white hands, dead white against his trousers. Then he will say, "Everyone says it is wonderful to live to an old age. Everyone wants to be able to grow old." He shrugs. A hidden tear comes to the corner of his eye and begins to make a warm path down the cold cheek. "They say it's fine to live long. And I say, 'For what?'"

We see the years chiseled in the features of the old man. We know that age has laid a painful knapsack on his curved shoulders. But "old" is an evanescent term, a quicksilver word, holding various meanings for various human beings.

Aging may take place in a number of ways. Primary aging

is the state which occurs as one grows older and functions decline. Everyone knows what it is to lose the capacity for some activity. The forty-year-old man who finds himself soundly beaten by a thirty-year-old companion on the tennis court is aware that his body does not respond with the same strength and speed that it once did. The middle-aged woman who plans and executes a large party at home finds that one night's rest does not restore her or erase her fatigue. The baseball player who is considered "old" at thirty knows that "aging" has many facets.

Secondary aging is perhaps less well understood. Here disease or injuries may make biological aging occur faster. Persons who have serious diseases, strokes, or debilitating injuries experience secondary aging. Also, scientists are trying to learn more about biological aging and may obtain some of their information from a strain of Norwegian dogs which mature in a time span which might be compared to human childhood. A project at Indiana University School of Medicine funded by the U.S. Public Health Service and the Children's Brain Diseases Foundation in San Francisco is studying generations of English Setters who suffer from a particular disease which turns them into old animals in a period of months. The dogs are helping scientists understand not just the disease of aging but the normal processes of aging in humans. The team has agreed on a description of aging as a "dark-brown stain that spreads. . . ." The color of old age is in granules of pigment which accumulate in the cells of the liver, the heart, the brain, and central nervous system, sometimes the eyes. These cells do not divide and replace themselves as do most others.[2] The dogs, which often die of old age by the time they are two, are teaching much about the process of aging in humans and about the rare disease which sometimes attacks children and forces them to age before they have become adults. Because many generations of dogs can be studied in the span of relatively few years, scientists hope to achieve a breakthrough by discovering the causes of this type of aging and then perhaps in learning how the process itself can be reversed.

Psychological age takes place in an entirely different way. Some people are psychologically old in their twenties, others psychologically young in their eighties. Attitudes toward new experiences; flexibility concerning change; curiosity about experiences; humor concerning events—all of these influence the psychological age of a person.

The capacity to learn is included as an index of psychological age, and what might be added is the curiosity to want to learn. Although memory may be less reliable than it was in an earlier age, persons who stay in the learning pattern, at colleges or on the job or at home, find that they can compensate for the lack of recall of specific names or events by their interest and overall ability to think through problems or to evaluate events.

Psychological age is measured in terms of what a man is, how he experiences life. The psychologically young seem to have no "cutoff valve" to life but continue to feel and experience and be a part of living.

Finally, social age becomes that age which is gauged by social roles and habits. Forced retirement at 65 makes a social role definition of old age. The cutoff points of putting members of various social clubs into other categories at certain ages make for a routine role definition of aging for those people.

The social role, then, is that which is most often seen in the eyes of other people whose opinions one values. In defining mental health, Bonaro Overstreet once said that it could be defined not by what it was intrinsically but by what others became in one's presence. The characterization of one's social role in the older years might be similar. How others respond to the person who has retired may help to define his social role in society.

The diminution of the social role has been stated thus by Ruth Cavan:

. . . the man is a lawyer without a case, a bookkeeper without books, a machinist without tools . . . he is excluded from his group of former co-workers . . . as retired person, he begins to find a different evaluation of himself in the minds of others from the evaluation he had as an employed person. He no longer sees respect in the eyes of former subordinates, praise in the face of former superiors, and approval in the manner of former co-workers. The looking glass composed of his former important groups throws back a changed image: he is done for, an old-timer, old-fashioned, on the shelf.[3]

Thus, one can see that the determination of who is old may be made in a number of different ways, depending on who is doing the determining. The interlocking forces of man's internal makeup plus his developed attitudes toward life and his physical strength and endurance all work together to shape his existence and to work for or against him as he lives.

The "problems of aging" have grown directly from medical progress in helping people live longer, and the question now often becomes not one of how a person may live longer but for what?

When is a person old?

For Mary Thompkins, social leader, it happened during her daughter's freshman year in college. Trim Mary—tennis-playing, party-giving, club-going—looked into the lighted makeup mirror one morning and saw deepening lines from nose to mouth, shadow of other creases around her eyes, and three new gray hairs. The thought of "going sustaining" in the Junior League because of her fortieth birthday overtook her. She began to cry and to curse the forties which brought with them diminution in energy, in looks, and in appeal.

When is a person old?

For Harrison Caldwell old age was still a future shadow on his eightieth birthday. Although he had retired (and had the gold watch to prove it) when he was 65, the lumber company which he had served still used him as a consultant several days a month. Besides, he kept up his golf game and volunteered to help several young parolees. Life was not the same since Frances had died, leaving him the big house and empty rooms. But he worked at making retirement pleasant as hard as he had worked at his job, and he found most days sweetened with small successes and good encounters.

When is a person old?

Perhaps it is when he first feels unwanted or unneeded, or when the awareness first strikes that new generations are taking over his activities or his dreams.

Old age for most people lies in loss of status. The institutionalized aged, sitting bleak on straight-backed chairs, bear witness that the "new generation" of older people are too often forced to measure existence by body functions rather than soul-fulfillments.

Gone for the most part are the autumn days of rural life where children took root close to the farms of the parents and multifamilies grew like spring grain around the older couple. Gone are the many hands which helped with planting and with harvesting; no longer are there "kitchen lessons" where canning and apple-pie making were demonstrated. The firm philosophy spoken, skills taught, and examples set have been replaced by a culture in which few men see the results of the products they help to make and where artificial goods and programs have replaced the natural methods employed by earlier generations.

When populations grew slowly, human beings were precious commodities. Only about five million people inhabited the world some 10,000 years ago, fewer than now live in the Chicago metropolitan area. As agriculture was developed, death rates fell. Medical knowledge improved, and death rates dropped still further. Reduction in birth rates helped somewhat, and developed countries now grow at an average rate of one percent per year. However, in less developed countries where medical technology came into practice without serious efforts at teaching birth control, growth is at about 2.5 percent, doubling every thirty years or so.[4]

With the stress which growing populations put on this planet, it is easy to see why, psychologically, older people are often regarded as burdens.

In a "now" generation, old people can soon feel obsolete. Cars, television sets, houses, and refrigerators change models on almost an annual basis. If built-in obsolescence is the order of the day, the "phasing out" of people may well be part of the subtle agenda of the times. Mandatory retirement, nuclear families, and small living units do not allow for the expansion of older people into the extended family pattern of earlier times. The job market holds tight against the older worker; and urban living with its speed, freeways, and complex shopping and traffic patterns may all work against the older person who seeks independence.

What are the lessons from Harrison Caldwell or, negatively, from Mary Thompkins which may act on behalf of the person who feels the sun of youth on his back?

The person who reaches 60 or 70 or 80 in a state of reasonable health carries within him the person he was at 25 or 30 or 40. The weight of responsibilities or energies or desires may have shifted, but he maintains the knowledge and feelings, desires and dislikes, similar to those characteristic of the person he was before. Perhaps this lesson is the most important to be learned.

What determines the process of aging? Physical factors, of course, play a vital part. But mental attitudes may cast an even longer shadow. The equating of retirement with leisure; the concept of aging as a period of inactivity; the outlook of older years as empty ones—all of these help to further a mode of life which demonstrates that "old" is useless. Young children "catch" the attitude from their parents and grow up to demonstrate to their children that old cars should be traded in and old people should be put aside.

Who bears the responsibility for many of the current attitudes about aging? The younger generation, or the older people themselves? Studies in school classes have shown that there is a "self-fulfilling prophecy" which demonstrates that a person becomes what he is expected to be. The misbehaving child, the "different" youngster, the slow learner will often become more of what his teacher expects as the weeks go on. So is it with us all. The cherished human being is able to cherish others; the person who knows respect can give it to himself and to those around him. Conversely, the man or woman who is expected to be nonproductive or withdrawn may well shrink into the image which is set for him.

The responsibility for aging productively, then, becomes the concern of the persons at retirement age. However, it is also important to their children, their grandchildren, and the generations after them.

Aging, then, is complex—yet simple. Some facets of the process are controlled externally. Heredity, health, and accident are factors no one can alter. Societal factors such as retirement practices cannot be manipulated by single individuals, but they can be changed by the prolonged and concerted efforts of many. However, the psychological factors of aging remain the ones which all people can study and endeavor to mold. Development of the qualities of curiosity, flexibility, and wonder helps people to retain youthful attributes and to give the passing years changing but positive meaning.

We have seen that people regard age at different times and in different ways. Yet, just as no one can stop a baby from developing into a child and then an adult, so no one can halt the years by magic potions or surgery or exercise. The circular effect of life is demonstrated in the changing seasons, rotation of the moon, and symbol of the wedding band. It is demonstrated again in the rounding of the life-span from birth to death.

Perhaps the continuing studies concerning aging may bring new knowledge and longer spans of living. Until that time the vital aspect of living longer years lies in the ability to make them meaningful and productive to oneself and to others.

SOME FIGURES

Today, as these words are being read, approximately 4,000 Americans reached their sixty-fifth birthday. About 3,000 died, leaving an additional 1,000 people who attained the artificial aging mark. Approximately one in ten Americans is 65 or older. In the 1970 census 20,049,592 Older Americans were counted out of a total of 203,165,699 residents.[5] These figures contrast with the 1900 census, which showed 3.1 million older persons out of 76 million residents, a total of 4.1 percent or one person in 25.

By the year 2000 it is estimated that there will be at least 28 million persons 65 and over in the United States.

Reports from the 1970 census show that the older population of 65 and over grew faster than the remaining population (21.1 percent vs. 12.5 percent). For those 75 and over, the percentage increase was even greater (37.1 percent vs. 13 percent). Also, the number of older women grew faster than the number of older men (28.6 percent vs. 12.1 percent).

The proportion of the 203.2 million United States residents in the years of 45 to 64 increased from 20.1 percent to 20.6 percent. The total middle-aged and older population came to 61.8 million or 31.5 percent of all Americans, almost one in three.

In the one hundred years since 1870, the total population has become five times as large, the middle-aged population nine times as large, and the older population 17 times as large.[6]

In numbers the older population represents a number equaling the total population of all ages of our 21 smallest states. In age they vary from just 65 to more than 125.

The 1970 census showed 11.6 million older women but only 8.4 million older men. Most older men are married; most older women are widowed.

Of the males between 65 and 74, 7.3 percent are single, 78.7 percent married, 11.5 percent widowed, and 2.5 percent divorced. The men 75 years and over show similar percentage ratings: 5.6 percent are single, 59.3 percent married, 33.1 percent widowed, and 2 percent divorced.

Females between 65 and 74 are widowed in greater numbers, 43.8 percent. Single females are 7.3 percent; married, 46.1; and divorced, 2.7 percent. In the 75 and older age bracket, the single rate rises to 8.2 percent, the married drops to 19.3, and the widowed soars to 71 percent. Divorce accounts for 1.5 percent.[7]

How do these older people live? And where? Most of them, statistics show, remain in some type of family setting. An increasing proportion maintain households of their own. About one fourth live alone, most of them women, a reflection of the greater number of older women than older men. Only one in 20 exists in an institution.[8]

Most older people live in the Middle Atlantic states, followed closely by the East North Central area, and then by the South Atlantic states, including Florida.[9]

For the most part, older Americans follow the pattern for the total population and live in the larger states. More than one fourth of the over-65-year-old group live in California, New York, and Pennsylvania. With the addition of Illinois, Ohio, and Texas, we find that 40.4 percent of the older people and 40.8 percent of the total population reside in those six states. If four more states are included, Florida, Michigan, New Jersey, and Massachusetts, we have 55.8 percent of the over-65-year-old group and 54.8 percent of total population.

Thus, we find that the 21 smallest states contain only 10 percent of the older population.[10]

About 40 percent of persons 65 and over are in nonmetropolitan areas, and only 5 percent live on farms, the other 35 percent living in towns. For those who stay in metropolitan areas, most of the older people live in the city itself, while the majority of younger people are in the suburbs.[11]

In the labor force the proportion of older people continues to drop. In 1900 almost two thirds of older men were working. In 1970 the proportion was just a bit over one in four. Many men have begun to retire early; and, while the participation of older women in paid work has gone from about 8 percent in 1900 to 10 percent in 1970, older workers of both sexes find difficulty in being hired in any job once they become unemployed.

Even though there are many wealthy aged people, the older group is mainly a low-income one. Of the 7.2 million families with heads of 65 or over in 1970, half had incomes of less than $5,053. The picture is even grimmer for the single older person. Of the 5.8 million of them living alone or with nonrelatives, half had incomes of less than $1,951, less than half of that of the under-65 individuals.[12]

In 1952, with 12 million people 65 and over, one in six received monthly Social Security checks. Today, of the 20 million older people, four out of five receive Social Security checks. For most people Social Security payments have become the largest single share of their income, now about 34 percent.

As for housing, although almost two thirds of older Americans own their own houses (and about 8 in 10 are mortgage-free), the increased taxes are making it more difficult for people in the older age bracket to stay in their homes. Apartment living may not appeal, or high rents may make such moves unfeasible. Senator Harrison A. Williams stated that although about 350,000 housing units have been made available through federal programs in the last 10 years, they total only the average net gain among persons 65 or older in the nation every year. In addition, about six million of the older Americans live in housing which is substandard.[13]

For those who have endured life in substandard jobs or

housing—the disadvantaged—the problem is greater. The average of those older people living in poverty or near poverty
in 1970 was about 21.9 percent of families with white male
heads and almost 57.6 percent for those with Negro female
heads. For the older people living by themselves or with non-
related persons, the average of those living in poverty was 60
percent overall. However, of the white males, the average
was 47.8 percent and for the Negro females, 88.3 percent.[14]

THE SUBTLE PROBLEMS OF AGING

The multitudinous problems faced by older people are suc-
cinctly stated by T. V. Smith as follows, "Why worry about a
falling star in a rising world? But the doctors won't let us
older people die, short of suicide; and the theologians won't
let us commit suicide with dignity and proper peace of mind
. . . we aged must keep on being. . . . But we are anomalous
even as we grow more numerous." [15]

Dr. Smith continues with the dilemma of the aged by
saying, "It is that we lack a philosophy which makes old age
respectable and which would prevent the normal process of
decay and death from appearing as a surd in the life of reason." [16]

The types of depression which many older people suffer
and the high rate of suicide among the aged are explained by
many authorities as pain which they endure from multiple
bereavements. Because he is unlikely to be able to replace
many of the losses which he bears, the older person is unable
to bear the deaths of persons close to him. Also, the fact that
losses may occur rapidly keeps the person from finishing his
"grief work." As death follows death, the person suffering
may be unable to respond to the new loss because he is still
mourning for the old one.

Sometimes when the grief is beyond his power to endure,
he may, when he cannot work out his sorrow verbally or emotionally, substitute a preoccupation with bodily symptoms.

He will cease investing emotionally in other people, silently stating that he does not want to care again for someone who might leave him. Thus he begins withdrawing from life and people and moving into himself.

The elderly person who cannot handle his multiple losses and attendant grief may commit suicide. As Earl A. Grollman has said, "Year in and year out, the older people rank at the bottom of the list for suicide threats and attempts. Annually, they top the statistics of those whose suicide has been completed." [17] Mr. Grollman goes on to say that a British study of suicide among the aged showed that the suicidal persons had demonstrated chronic feelings of discouragement, loss of general competence, and a major shift of self-image. He states that "ingredients vital to the morale of people of all ages—love, caring, and understanding—are so often forgotten when elderly people are concerned." [18] Often illness of the older person is a triggering factor.

The incidence of suicide is highest in the aged in our country, and suicide itself is the eleventh leading cause of death.[19] Further, "There is a decade-by-decade rise of depression, including the peaking of the suicide rate in men in their eighties. Twenty-five percent of all suicides occur in persons over 65 years of age." [20]

An old person can "commit suicide" conversely by failing to care for himself, to eat properly, to seek medical attention when it is indicated. He may even cease his bodily movements and activities in order to allow himself to worsen physically.

Another symptom is that he may turn his negative and unhappy feelings into hostile reactions to other people. As he relates unpleasantly to others, they often move away from him, thus compounding the problems from which he suffers.

The idea of multiple bereavements and the attendant reactions experienced by the old gives a new perspective to the character changes which go on in older people. Instead of

being irreversible processes of aging, some of them may occur
as a result of the unhappiness and suffering which have come
from losses of loved ones in rapid succession.

Myths concerning older people abound. "People cannot
learn after the age of fifty." "Old people shouldn't be trying
to hold down jobs." "Sex? It's nonexistent in the older years."
Swaddled in the binding myths, many older people try to
conform to the image portrayed in the popular literature.
They join a Golden Age Club and spend a half day a week
playing dominoes. They invest in a bigger television set and
move their lives from inside their being to the projection of
dots on the screen before them. And in bed they make truth
of folk lore. Kisses are plastic touches on mouth or cheek; no
fires are permitted to light or burn.

And so unhappiness is created in the image of the myth.
Wilma Donahue points out that cerebral capacity begins to
weaken only in later years and then relatively slowly. "Maturity of fifty years," the author says, "brings with it judgment,
a consciousness of the magnitude of the world and the place
of the individual in it, and increased opportunity for self-expression and pursuit of knowledge. . . . The human mental
machine is now, at last, ready for its prime performance." [21]

People can't learn in later years? Look at college enrollments, especially in areas of continuing education. Older people constantly flaunt the myth that learning ceases early.
Thousands of people are earning degrees, or taking noncredit
courses for pleasure, developing new leisure-time skills, or attending college classes for the mental stimulation obtained
there.

Perhaps most damaging to the self-image of the person
grown older are the false ideas that sex dies when the retirement age comes. If the wish is father to the child, the belief is
also often parent to the action (or nonaction).

Research by Dr. William H. Masters and Mrs. Virginia E.
Johnson has demonstrated that under suitable physical and
emotional conditions the capacity to enjoy sex remains at any

age. Like other functions of existence it may slow down grad-
ually. The Masters and Johnson studies have demonstrated
that there is no "cutoff point" for sexual activity, just as there
is no definite stopping point for intellectual stimulus.[22]

The reinvestment of feelings is important for persons who
have grown older. If immediate family is removed, then there
are others who may be able to provide emotional satisfaction.

A continuing fact emerges. The person who has learned to
cope with stress, to meet problems, and to maintain emotional health in youth develops skills to cope with similar
problems in later years. Aging as a continuum of the coping
mechanism can be learned from childhood.

Early joys and skills, ability to live fully and ably—these
may well be the underpinnings for the building of an older
life of continuing pleasure and reward.

The "problems" of aging are sociological, psychological,
financial, and physical. So are the "problems" of everyone.
From the pink infant mewing toothlessly in the hospital nursery to the octogenarian on the next floor sighing (also toothlessly) in her bed lie the whole spectrum of life and the endless cycle of beginnings and endings.

The babies side by side in their cribs may be potential gen-
iuses, retardates, criminals, lifesavers. The old people dying
may leave a heritage of love or bitterness, knowledge or igno-
rance. The older people represent the potential and promise,
the fulfillment and the emptiness which are part of each of
us. They are not "better than" or "worse than" we are. They
are the same as we are.

When nations are in conflict, the adversary becomes "the
guerrilla" or "the enemy" or "the troops killed." Such labels
remove the human quality from the killing and permit
bloodshed without horror and without grief.

In *The Prophet*, Kahlil Gibran writes of death, "You would
know the secret of death, but how shall you find it unless you
seek it in the heart of life? . . . If you would indeed behold
the spirit of death, open your heart wide unto the body of

life. For life and death are one, even as the river and the sea are one." [23]

In regarding older people also it is important to remember that childhood, adulthood, and aging are part of one continuum called "life." If we want to see how a community treats its older people, we have only to look at how it treats its infants, children, poor, mentally ill, and others, for each of them is part of the culture of the community. Each contributes to the emotional climate of that town.

An experiment made by Lee Salk of City Hospital in Elmhurst, New York, demonstrated what a sense of security could mean even to a newborn infant. Using 102 babies for the experiment and a matched group for controls, he had a recording made with nothing on it but the sound of a mother's heartbeat—72 paired beats per minute.

When findings were recorded, it was discovered that the experimental infants gained more weight, although both groups had the same amount of nourishment offered. The experimental babies cried about half as much as the control ones, although nothing was added to the experimental group but a sound which was associated with closeness to the mother in utero. [24]

If it is true that aging is but an expansion of the other experience of life, some lessons might be learned from the foregoing experiment. Removing old people from the "heart" of life, from the sound of activities, from the feeling of being in the midst of purposeful movement is to isolate them into a "control" group tagged with the label of "old and forgotten." The older person needs to be seen in all his many roles—as part of the community "heart," as citizen, voter, family member, church-goer, potential volunteer.

If we are going to look at the aged people in this culture, really look, and really see, we shall remove the labels and begin to view the people with all of their needs and eccentricities, their furies and their delights, their potential and their emptiness. We shall begin to see men and women who have lived more years than are before them and who share the hopes of each of us—that the time remaining can be lived with meaning.

We are speaking of the aged. Kahlil Gibran once said, "Should you really open your eyes and see, you would behold your image in all images. And should you open your ears and listen, you would hear your own voice in all voices." [25] In the aged we see ourselves, with our goodness and our prejudices, with our love and our loneliness.

CHAPTER TWO

Needs We Share

Human beings of all ages may be united by similarities or separated by differences. Yet no matter how many disparities exist in their ages, states, or backgrounds, they share many similar needs.

All people of all ages have the psychological desire for relatedness, meaning, sexuality, and self-acceptance. In addition, they require certain physical aids in order to function. Without adequate health, nutrition, and income, they are locked within a prison where the psychological needs may atrophy.

This chapter will examine some of the requirements, both psychological and physical, which bind together people of every age. The narrow band of similarities which ties men one to the other often seems invisible within the boundaries of the differences. Yet now let us uncover some common needs which belong to each human being.

PSYCHOLOGICAL NEEDS

The need for relatedness may well be the greatest force propelling all men.

Clark Tibbitts has suggested the five needs which should be satisfied if persons are to grow maturely:

1) *the need for relatedness, or association with others;*
2) *the need for creativity;*
3) *the need for security;*
4) *the need for individuality, or recognition; and*
5) *the need for orientation or an intellectual frame of reference.*[1]

"Relatedness," which Tibbitts places first, has to do with all human relationships—those which take place in the family and at work, in organizations, and in the larger world which people share. Relatedness has to do with humanness and all the activities with other human beings in the universe. Such a sense of relatedness is removed from people who are taken from their life tasks of work, participation, homemaking, or family membership and are placed in a setting where their physical wants are looked after while their human needs are allowed to atrophy.

If therapists were to be polled concerning what they consider the greatest tragedy which can befall human beings, they might well respond with "the sense of aloneness." As Erich Fromm forcefully states it, "The deepest need of man, then, is the need to overcome his separateness, to leave the prison of his aloneness. The *absolute* failure to achieve this aim means insanity. . . ."[2]

Dr. Fromm explains that the feeling of separateness is anxiety-arousing because being separate means being unable to use one's humanness. For the very old the sense of separateness may be compounded by the sad recognition that not only is one remote from other human beings at this moment in life but that death may soon cover the final vestige of the humanness or existence of the person.

No one wants to be a footstep planted in the sand near the rushing sea, a footprint to be washed away into eternal waters, a sign seen for an instant and then erased forever. The sense of identity with other loving creatures; a sense of belonging to the human endeavor or being a part of creative movement; a realization that one's life has counted to some-one else—these have to be realized by persons growing older. If they cannot find themselves as a permanent part of life, then they will surely lose themselves in a desperate living death.

Not all old people can verbalize their feelings. Not all of them recognize why they have such a sense of desolation and depression. Yet many have seen the slow dissolution of their life's investment in both people and tasks without the re-placement of other duties or attachments.

They have a close resemblance to the mentally ill who, un-able to bear the pain which life has dealt them, withdraw all the way into themselves where they can use the protective coating of denial and forgetfulness against the lash of reality and aloneness which they feel. They sit in a constant twilight without the skills or ability to find the light of companionship or relatedness which could bring them into meaning once again.

Where do most older persons obtain satisfactions? What brings them happiness? These questions have been asked over the years. Studies have been undertaken to help provide answers.

One such study reported by Christine M. Morgan at-tempted to discover factors related to good adjustment in the elderly. The people examined were noninstitutionalized older persons from a variety of backgrounds living in a general community setting.[3]

One particular finding reported from the survey was that there is no one guideline or description of an "old person." The traits which the older people demonstrated were as var-ied as are those shown by any sampling of populations of vari-ous age groups.

When the older people were asked what gave them great-est happiness in their early lives, they ranked family and fam-ily relationships at the top of the list. Conversely, in stating what they missed most from their earlier years, they placed deceased members of the family first, demonstrating once again that relationship to life, companionship with others, and a sense of being needed and loved were the qualities which elderly persons considered essential to happiness.

Additionally, the main differential meaningful activity between the group which considered itself the happiest and the one who felt unhappiest was in the amount of work and meaningful activity which they had to do. The happiest group, it was demonstrated, was the busiest.

In the final analysis, older people asked for economic security. But more than that, they asked for work to do and people with whom to relate. They demonstrated that their needs and wishes were the same as those of persons in any age group and that they counted their days in terms of participation and involvement rather than in hours or in years.

Speaking at a meeting of the World Federation for Mental Health in London, Dr. Leon Eisenberg said, "Songbirds cannot sing in isolation." No bird can; nor can any human being.

In discussing the anonymity suffered by many people in our culture, Rollo May states that the severest punishment which Yahweh could inflict on his people was to blot out their names. He says, "Loneliness and its stepchild, alienation, can become forms of demon possession. Surrendering ourselves to the impersonal daimonic pushes us into an anonymity which is also impersonal." [4]

Dr. May uses the examples in speaking of young people in our culture, but the example applies only too aptly to the old. For many of them who feel "used" or useless and most especially forgotten, the loneliness which they inherit is a pervasive and overriding part of life.

Sexuality

Americans live in a sexual world. The lithe and lovely young woman running up the hill with an athletic bronze-skinned male evokes in us feelings of delight and envy. Advertisements entice one to try a certain perfume or spray or after-

shave lotion (guaranteed to send members of the opposite sex
heading toward you). Department stores advertise sheer
nightgowns or see-through blouses. Songs plaintively tell of
love and need. Movies abound with dramas of sexual pursuits. Novels about sex hit the best seller list. Books concerning lovemaking between two robust adults are popular.

That sex is here to stay is the message which comes
through. However, there is a hidden proviso. Sex is for the
young. Few if any advertisements show older couples in
loving embrace—unless those ads are for life insurance or
prepaid funeral arrangements!

Small wonder, then, that older people soon have the idea
that sex, like childbearing, has its season and then is removed
from a life pattern. One has only to read the popular "letters"
in most newspapers to find out that one partner of a long-
standing marriage is puzzled or unhappy because sex has
been outlawed by the other. Women who have gone through
menopause or men who experience failure a time or two are
often prone to decide that "sex is over."

The thoughts of sexual relations between persons in their
fifties or sixties or beyond often seem ludicrous or repulsive in
this youth-bound culture. Because such taboos have been
present, very little, until recently, has been known with accu-
racy about the sex lives of older people. Young persons were
mostly uninterested, and older ones were slightly ashamed to
discuss the matter even with their physicians.

Recent studies have opened doors to information about the
process of living as well as of loving. As the findings have
been reported, the silence about middle- and older-aged sex
has been broken. Additionally, many of the accompanying
guilt feelings which old people had about their sexual interests have been diminished and have been replaced by an
awareness that to be a living human being is to be a sexual
person and that such feelings and impulses are no more inappropriate in later years than are appetites for food or hunger
for fine music or literature.

The "new enlightenment" which results in free discussion of sex among people, in literature, or on the screen may be having its carryover in a more open discussion of older people and their attitudes. The guilt which adolescents have often felt because of their sexual desires may well have had its counterpart in the older persons who tried to suppress their needs and wishes and who suffered silent anguish because of them. To be an old person without feelings of sexuality is to be a selfless old person. At all ages and at any age a person has to have the awareness of his own role and place among his peers and within himself. Everyone at any age is a sexual creature. Does that sound strange? It should not, for human sexuality is a vital factor in life. It may or may not relate to sex per se, but it does definitely relate to a person's conception of himself, his masculinity or femininity, his "place" in the universe.

Recent studies have shown some surprising findings to those who think of old age as a sexless wilderness where people have risen above the flesh and have lost desires for physical contact. Far from it. Interviews with people in retirement villages and apartments have showed that sexual activity, while less frequent or vigorous than that of youth, is much a part of the lives of many old people.

Dr. Francis J. Braceland sums up the problem thus:

The old person yearns for, needs, and desires the same satisfactions as the young, differing not in quality though somewhat in degree. Yet the culture has a bias against their expression. What is virility at 25 is lechery at 65. . . . Actually sex in later years correlates strongly with sex in earlier years. It is a timeless drive throughout life even in the 80s and 90s, especially if one's partner is alive.[5]

Studies by Dr. Alfred Kinsey have demonstrated that sexual capacities, particularly in women, showed little evidence of aging. Still other reports confirm the facts that a large percentage of men under seventy are capable of sexual relations, and one out of three of the men above seventy is still potent.

"Few factors play as important a part in bringing about impotence as does the fear of failure," says Isadore Rubin, who adds, "A temporary loss of desire or a temporary failure of potency may occur at any age. . . . When it occurs in the later years, . . . it may convince the male that 'this is it'—that he has reached the end of his sex life." [6]

The Masters and Johnson reports add that regularity of sexual performance is necessary for both males and females in order to maintain their responsiveness. Authorities feel that regular activity infused with variety will add to the older person's sex life. Couples are urged to use imagination in bringing to new life some sexual activities in their marriages.

The fear of using themselves up or of promoting a first or second heart attack has restrained many men from indulging in sex in later years. However, Dr. Eugene Scheimann disagrees with those who feel that sex can be damaging to an aging heart. On the contrary, Dr. Scheimann believes instead that sex releases tension and brings about increased good health by activating the thyroid, burning up cholesterol and calories, exercising muscles, and making the heart pump more blood for a short period and then relax.

"A healthy night of sex," says Dr. Scheimann, "is nature's tranquilizer, reducing stress and creating a general feeling of relaxation and well-being." [7] His statement is strengthened by the opinion of other physicians who recommend that men can well indulge in sexual activities after prostate operations or heart attacks.

Dr. Scheimann further promotes his original position by stating that in his opinion men with sexual frustrations are more prone to heart disease than those without them.

The fears of ridicule or failure which have impeded many persons in their later years from indulging in the "foolishness" of sex may be reduced on large scale as more of the findings about sexual activity are made public. Women some-times hold back because their own image of self-attractive-ness is diminishing and because they do not imagine that they can be appealing to any man. Men often cease trying to en-gage in sexual activities if they experience failure or if their wives seem uninterested or disdainful. However, when a cou-ple is able to maintain a loving attitude toward one another and when their emotional experiences are generally good and supportive, they seem to be able to enjoy sex as an outreach of their natural expressions of affection for one another.

The mandatory age of retirement has, in this culture, had its mandatory counterpart in sexual restraint, a taboo which may well have its effect on the lives of thousands of older people.

The "self-fulfilling" prophecy has been described in class-rooms where teachers reported improvement in pupils who had been predicted to make spectacular growth in a semes-ter. Not knowing that the children were picked at random, the teachers demonstrated their own expectation for growth, and the children responded.

The same type of "self-fulfilling" prophecy can work so far as older people are concerned. When the synthetic male sex hormone testosterone was first introduced at Johns Hopkins Hospital in Baltimore, a 55-year-old man who received an in-jection reported that his waning sexual power was revived immediately afterwards. The next time the same man re-quested an injection, he was given one of sterile oil from a bottle labeled "testosterone." On each occasion he reported that the subsequent injections were just as powerful as the first.

This prediction of failure or of success can work between people. The wife who insists that her husband is too old for sex or the husband who is convinced that his sex life is over can well make truth of fear or fallacy.

The myth that masturbation is evil or that it should be reserved for the young is also dispelled by the experts who feel that masturbation is a perfectly valid outlet for gaining release from sexual tensions.

Simone de Beauvoir states that "An inquiry into the sexuality of the aged amounts to asking what happens to a man's relationship with himself, with others, and with the outside world when the pre-eminence of the genital aspect of the sexual pattern has vanished." [8]

In the findings reported by Simone de Beauvoir, it is demonstrated that manual workers seem to have more straightforward desires than those of the middle class and are more likely to fulfill them at any age.

The very sophistication of society and the taboos put upon people often serve as restrictions to activity which might give release to older persons. The societal secrecy about sex in later years and the attendant feelings of guilt which result on the part of older persons with sexual needs often compound problems and lead to psychological difficulties.

Dr. Harvey L. Gochros in an article urges social workers to help elderly people develop social contacts through clubs and organizations. He goes on to point out that sex education might be useful. Then he makes the following radical suggestion: "Perhaps we might even consider the long-range prospect of marital reform for the aged. Such reform would acknowledge the far greater number of aged women than men and therefore legalize polygamous living arrangements for those past 65." [9]

Although Dr. Gochros' idea is not likely to be accepted by large numbers of people, the problem posed by his article is a real one which will not disappear by ignoring it. Many older women live alone. They are human beings with human needs. It might be helpful simply to help them recognize their desires for what they are, to acknowledge that human needs are not intrinsically evil, and to aid them in finding outlets through fantasy or masturbation as releases from sexual tension.

The people who have been married happily and who have known the joys of physical contact with a mate are likely to feel the greatest need after the acute grief period over the mate's death has passed. In this culture, instead of recognizing the need as a tribute to the emotional responsiveness stimulated by the loving relationship, we often penalize by our disapproving attitudes the persons feeling such desires.

The happier and richer the sexual life has been, the longer it continues, reports de Beauvoir. For older men, the indirect forms of satisfaction which come about from reading or engaging in fantasies may take precedence over the physical act of sex, even when the man is not impotent. However, what is confirmed here is exactly what other studies have found concerning elderly men, that sexual life "depends on their past and also upon their attitude toward their old age as a whole and toward their image in particular." [10]

For women, sex lives may well be both more stable and more lasting. The studies of Masters and Johnson confirmed that a woman can still reach orgasm at any age and can find pleasure in lovemaking even if she does not have orgasm from it. Despite that fact, the Kinsey studies showed that women have a less active sex life than men. The statistical number of older women who are widows and the cultural factors which keep women from having love affairs plus the fact that old women are often regarded as undesirable keep the aging single woman from finding outlets in normal sexual activities.

What, then, do these findings show? Many studies about physical aging have demonstrated that people are not slotted into "stages" or "ages" but that all human beings move along a continuum of development or decline and that various phases of activity or body functioning change at different rates. However, unless there is severe deterioration of the brain, the humanness of people remains throughout the lifespan. To be a human being is to be a sexual creature. To know one's masculinity or one's femininity is to be aware of one's place in the universe. It has been said that there exists a strong bond between creativity and sexuality. Perhaps the link between them is the feeling of being alive, a part of the universe, a seeing, feeling, loving human being who can reach out to and respond to others. The person who knows his place within himself, who feels his own worthwhileness, is then able to be a creative part of the larger world in which he lives.

PHYSICAL NEEDS (HEALTH)

Aging may, like Mark Twain's weather, be more often discussed than acted upon in a meaningful manner. Many people speak of aging; few define what it is they mean. As we look at the similarities in needs among older persons, we find that physical health ranks among the highest necessities.

Perhaps a short look at physical aging and the biologic mechanism may help to put into perspective this discussion of health needs. Wilma Donahue states that the aging process is continuous and consists of a decrease of tissue elasticity, decrease in ability of cells to divide and thus repair the normal wear in use or restoration of body tissue, decrease in all other factors that protect the physical well-being of the individual. She describes the physical and functional age changes which man undergoes but stresses that aging is a natural phenomenon and not one to be confused with disease.[11]

Hans Selye, a man who has devoted much of his adult life to a study of stress, calls stress "a kind of 'speedometer of life.'" He goes on to say that "vitality is like a special kind of bank account, which you can use up by withdrawals but cannot increase by deposits. Your only control over this most precious fortune is the rate at which you make your withdrawals."[12]

Dr. Selye feels that the goal of life is not to avoid stress, which, in moderation, is necessary for life; but the secret seems to be in finding what is one's own optimum stress-level and then keeping within it. Dr. Selye emphasizes the necessity for equalizing stress throughout one's being, stating that people die because one vital part of their bodies has worn out too early in proportion to the remainder. The two great limiting factors to anyone, according to Dr. Selye, are the supply of adaptation energy and the wear and tear that the weakest vital part of one's body can tolerate.

Health needs of older people might well be charted by looking at some of the statistics concerning chronic disabling conditions. Figures compiled by the National Health Survey show that two out of five older persons are limited by chronic conditions, in contrast to one in twenty under age 45.[13] The most common disabling conditions were heart disease, arthritis, rheumatism, visual impairments, hypertension, and mental and nervous disorders.

A combination of acute and chronic conditions restricted the activity of persons over 65 for almost five weeks out of the year, and two of the examples represented bed stays.

Although accidents did not happen as frequently to older people as to younger ones, they accounted for more disability days for the people over 65. About one in every six suffered some kind of injury during the year, one requiring medical attention and at least one day of disability. Two out of three of these occurred in the home.

During the one year reflected in these figures, more than one in five persons aged 65 or over had had some short-term stay in a hospital. This figure compares with only one in seven for persons in the 45–64 age group. Medical care in general was more frequently required by the older persons. The average number of visits to a doctor was 5.7, compared with 4.7 for the younger age group.

In a large number of the cases reported, the disabilities limited persons from following their normal pursuits, whether in working at a job or keeping house. Men reported a greater amount of limitation in their normal pursuit, a fact probably explained by the reality of men's working outside the home more frequently than women in that age group.

Good Health

The health needs of older people have to be among the first considerations, then, in any program which plans for ways in which to make the latter years of life meaningful and pleasurable. The restrictions which come with the other impingements of age, such as lack of meaningful employment and inability to drive a car, are then multiplied if the people so restricted are also limited seriously by health problems.

Any concern about the health of older people must take into account the many accidents which incapacitate them. Graham Blackstock reports on a study undertaken in Texas that the chief factor contributing to accidents is general debility, followed by illness and disease. The survey data showed that one out of every seven persons in the over–sixty-five population of Texas suffered injury from accident during the 12-month period of the survey. Although home was the place of occurrence of the largest number of accidents, streets and highways were the scene of the second-largest number.[14]

Since maintaining the health of older people is an important factor, more studies should be made concerning the accidents which the elderly encounter in order to see if preventive measures might be taken against the most frequent types of such accidents.

The "unnecessary depreciation" of people as they grow older is discussed by Edward J. Stieglitz, who states that the great majority of us are biologically older than our years.[15] Biologic time, determined by the rate of living, says Dr. Stieglitz, is an opposite equation to chronologic time. In examining the changes which occur with aging, Dr. Stieglitz states that repair after injury is slowed. His equation is that for every five years we have lived it takes an extra day to repair after a given injury. A second factor in the changes that happen with aging is that because symptoms of injury or illness become lessened with age, the older person is likely to wait too long to seek treatment or to report injury. Finally, according to Dr. Stieglitz, the reserves for stresses are lessened; and older people need to learn to avoid overexertion or extremes in eating habits or temperature exposures.

The responsibility of individuals for their own health is emphasized by Dr. Stieglitz, who feels that health is not a fundamental human right but instead is a privilege which requires responsibility on the part of the individual. He suggests that there should be preparation by education of youth on how to use the endowment of healthy bodies.

The physical aspects of aging interest researchers, and new studies are constantly underway concerning what makes people age. Nevertheless, any health knowledge is valueless unless it reaches the individual who can then act upon it. Increased nutritional knowledge on the part of people and physical checkups by physicians will go far toward helping older people maintain strength and health into the later years.

The difficulty with speaking of the physical needs of older people is that physical ailments are inextricably intertwined with psychological and social aspects of the aged person's life. This fact holds true much more for the person of advanced years than for the younger population.

Significant studies concerning the needs for a multifunctional assessment of elderly individuals have been made in a project conducted in Houston, Texas. Charles M. Gaitz and Paul E. Baer have reported that it is almost impossible to differentiate between the effects of aging and the effects of disease processes; ". . . the likelihood that a patient will have both physical and psychiatric illnesses, usually in combination with social problems, increases with age," the investigators state. They point out that in a multidisciplinary approach, it is recognized that each participating discipline may uncover impairments, disorders, or problems.[16]

The need to investigate a patient's environment as well as his physical health is stated as follows: "A mentally confused person with heart disease who lives in the home of an affluent, attentive daughter contends with different environmental stresses than one living alone or in a boarding house." Or, ". . . if a diagnosis of diabetes mellitus is made, the appraisal would still not be complete. One would also need to know if the patient can afford an adequate diet and if he has the capacity intellectually to follow a diet or administer insulin correctly." [17]

Finally, and maybe most importantly, they state, "Mental confusion in the elderly can be attributed to social isolation as well as to underlying heart or neural conditions." [18]

The investigators point out the reluctance of psychotherapists to consider intervention with an elderly patient because they often regard psychological problems as part of irreversible manifestations of aging. Case work with the elderly client is often undertaken reluctantly, and practitioners in various disciplines often do not communicate with one another or with the persons in social service agencies. If more than one medical opinion is needed, the elderly persons often do not have the financial resources or physical stamina to go from doctor to doctor. Even where there are information and referral services available for older people, there is almost never the sophisticated multifunctional orientation to help them obtain the entirety of needed services.

Responding to those who would delineate the financial cost of providing such multifunctional assessment services for older people, the investigators state that such assessment and subsequent meaningful care may well be balanced by savings in institutionalization and in the increased social participation of the older people themselves. They conclude their article by stating that there is serious need for further training of gerontologists and for inclusion of gerontological training in the traditional curricula.

The parallels seem obvious. Practitioners in well-baby clinics know that it is fruitless to prescribe procedures of cleanliness to the mother who does not have running water or who lives in a rat-infested tenement. They recognize that prescriptions for high-priced medicine or diets including milk, eggs, and cheese for little children may be not only impractical but impossible for the family existing on a poverty income and eating mostly starches and fats. By the same token, aged people who are alone or poor or confused—or a combination of all of those problems—cannot respond to a diagnosis of disability in any one area without facing needs in the other portions of his life. Prescriptions and diagnoses may be still other potions which are comfortable to give and nearly impossible to receive and act upon by that portion of our population whose problems are multiple and complex.

In order to provide necessary programs and aids for older people, varied resources need to be enlisted and many disciplines need to work together. Drs. Gaitz and Baer state that in making a functional assessment of elderly persons, the technician needs to recognize that they have a conglomerate of social, physical, and psychological problems and that their status is influenced by many factors.[19] They report, "In general, the likelihood that a patient will have both physical and psychiatric illnesses, usually in combination with social problems, increases with age." They feel that a multifunctional diagnostic appraisal as the basis for treatment of the elderly ill is necessary.

The writers acknowledge that each discipline may well uncover difficulties in the patient but that the final assessment has to be made on the basis of how one problem may impinge on another.

Yet knowing what is needed and providing it may be far different factors. Senator Edward Kennedy wrote of his horror that the American health care system is so callous to human suffering, so intent on high salaries and profits while being unconcerned about human needs.[20] The realities faced most especially by older people are that they and their families often live in ongoing fear because of the high costs of nursing facilities. Also, "over half of nursing home patients, of whom there are nearly a million, have some significant psychiatric symptoms or impairment, but mental health services are rare or nonexistent. National health insurance should properly cover the present areas of neglect and include the other mental health specialists." [21]

The multiple health and mental health difficulties suffered by the aged in our society are demonstrated in epidemiological studies. The incidence of psychiatric disorders is only one per 100,000 under 15 years of age, rising to 135 per 100,000 between 65 and 74 years of age, and 225 per 100,000 over 75 years of age.[22] Yet, "Many older people are turned away by state mental hospitals and by voluntary and municipal general hospitals because they are thought to be social emergencies which these institutions desire to exclude. Confused, wandering older people who are sent home by hospitals as senile and not ill are often in fact suffering from reversible brain condition caused by congestive heart failure, malnutrition, anemia, infections, and . . . [complications induced by] tranquilizers." [23]

The Group for the Advancement of Psychiatry, examining the problems of mental health needs of the elderly, emphasized the fact that the problem could not be understood simply in terms of numbers of people affected nor in the expenditures required. The chief problem, they reported, was "the continuing accumulation of untreated illnesses and disabilities" in our society.[24]

Numerous proposals concerning health care, insurance, and institutional facilities have been offered. However, no unified plan has yet resulted, and the older people in our society, particularly those who have little education or few financial resources, are often misplaced, misdiagnosed, or, even more tragically, untreated.

Good Nutrition

Good nutrition is taught in public school. Most children learn the value of green leafy vegetables, lean meat, and milk products. But the lessons learned may dissolve in the acid of old age as people lose resources or competences or companions.

Take Mrs. Lester. Loneliness keeps her from eating properly. She has money enough to purchase decent food, but ever since Harvey died and she moved, she has found food unpalatable and almost unnecessary. Her physician gives her tonics. Her friends comment on how bad she looks. But no one has yet taken the initiative to discover that Mrs. Lester is malnourished because she cannot or will not prepare for herself the broiled fish or baked chicken or crisp salad which might help to nourish her body and give her energy. Day by fading day she grows less energetic and more depressed.

That's not the case with Mr. Smith. He would eat decently if he had money enough for the food he wants. Ever since the company decided he was too old to drive the delivery truck, he's been trying to get along on his pension and his Social Security. They just don't buy him housing and clothes with money left over for the kind of food he likes. Mr. Smith spends a lot of time sitting by the window in his small apartment and watching people go by. He thinks about food a lot —about the steaks he used to get at the truck stop out of town or the fried chicken at the coffee shop near the warehouse or the fried ham and eggs at Maudie's Restaurant. Mr. Smith is hungry for a real meal.

Mrs. Channing would settle for Mr. Smith's scrambled eggs and ground beef. She doesn't even think of steaks or chicken anymore. She hardly remembers the days when she and Bill used to travel in the road shows and go into some all-night restaurant for Mexican food after the trapeze act was over. It seems as if it has been forever that she has lived in this little old hotel where the wallpaper bubbles or hangs down, revealing the faded scenes of earlier years. The tiny monthly check hardly pays her insurance (she wouldn't want to be buried like a pauper) or her once-a-month movie or the small cleaning bill or shoe repair. Her glasses haven't been changed for five years, and her eyes hurt. Mrs. Channing takes a small

basket when she goes grocery shopping. She would be humili-
ated if anybody she knew saw her buying cat food when they
know she has no pets. But Mrs. Channing has discovered that
cat food has some meat products and fish, and she cannot
afford to buy them any other way.

For Willie Washington it's still a different story. There isn't
much money, and she's getting too old to raise much decent
food in her garden. Willie is a big woman, and her cotton
dresses get tighter every year. It looks as if she's eating well
to be so fat. But her diet contains potatoes twice a day and
rice and noodles mixed with a little meat whenever she can
afford it. Of course, meat is hard to buy when you can't get
into town. Besides the old refrigerator is so warm that no
meat will keep for longer than 24 hours.

Gus Barrientos has lots of tortillas and pinto beans but very
little milk or green vegetables or meats. He doesn't complain,
but he doesn't feel well. The muscles which sustained him for
all his adult years (there were times when he could outwork
men half his age) have grown tired and disobedient. It even
hurts to get out of bed in the mornings, and his legs ache all
day long.

Mrs. Botts doesn't always remember to eat or to turn off
the stove if she is cooking something. Her landlady has
rushed in twice already to get a burned pot into the sink before it burst into flames. Mrs. Botts tries to keep herself nice
and well-fed. She doesn't want to be sent away to a home or
hospital, but she just can't always recall whether she has
eaten or not.

Frank Wellington still enjoys a good bit of roast beef or
steak—or would if he had the money to buy them and if his
dentures would permit him to chew the meat. It has been
fifteen years since he was fitted with his dentures, which are
now too loose to stay in place. Good nutrition for Frank is almost an impossibility, and he gets along as best he can on
foods which are soft and easy to swallow.

For all of these people whom we have just seen good nutritional practices are hampered by reasons of income, reduced activity, small appetite, or simply loneliness or unhappiness.

The physical elements of aging also can affect the eating habits of older people. For example, with aging comes a reduction of the basal metabolic rate which slows down the digestive process. Circulatory disturbances may also slow down the means for transporting nutrients from one part of the body to the other. Other physiological changes can also have bearings on how much older people eat.

Increasing knowledge of nutrition demonstrates what can happen to persons who do not have sufficient amounts of protein and other nutrients in their diets. Perhaps one of the most serious is the decreased resistance to infection. Mild anemia and lessened ability of the body to repair itself are also evidences of such insufficiency. Also, the body can lose protein when a person is inactive for long periods of time.

"The food was like ashes in my mouth." Those words have been said by many trying to eat under stress or under influence of grief. For the older person living alone the same reaction holds true. A sense of alienation or deep feeling of loneliness may well make food unpalatable. In addition, the trouble of preparing a hot meal may keep the single elderly person from cooking or eating anything more than a bowl of cereal or a sweet roll and tea or some quick hunger appeaser, no matter what its nutritional value.

Even when food is palatable and appealing, depression or loneliness can restrain people from eating. Consequently, many programs address themselves to the matter of providing hot meals in group settings, where conversation and companionship can be the seasoning which makes food even more appetizing.

Companionship, good nutrition, and mobility are tied together for many people. Thus, programs of providing hot noontime meals in groups also have built into them ways of transporting the older people to the centers where the meals are made available.

For the multitude of older people who are physically handicapped and who cannot leave their homes or beds or the many who are responsible for the care of others and cannot get away a pilot program entitled "Meals on Wheels" has been instituted. Here food is brought by volunteers on a once-a-day basis to the old person unable to prepare his own meals or to go where such meals are obtainable.

These projects touch only a small number of old people. There are the hidden old in roominghouses in the inner cities and those in shacks in the rural communities who suffer the worst of hunger pangs—that compounded by loneliness, fear, and physical needs.

Adequate Income

All of the needs listed are irrelevant unless the older person has an adequate income which will help him to a way of living with dignity and meaning. Many elderly persons in the 1970s have found themselves with "frozen" incomes at a time when rising costs of food, transportation, clothing, and taxes lessened their purchasing power.

Newspapers have carried many stories of old people, both men and women, who have died in their apartments, which were empty of food except for a few cans of soup or a loaf of bread. Always neighbors have expressed surprise that that "gentle Mrs. Ferguson" or that "nice Mr. Smith" should have been hungry or malnourished when they never complained.

The last act of dignity as a human being sometimes is to die hungry rather than to ask for help. That condition is one which has to be remedied.

The Bureau of Labor Statistics in 1970 suggested that the minimum standard of income adequacy for an elderly couple should be about $4,500 a year, with about 75 percent of that amount for a single person. In order to bring standards to that level, groups at the 1971 White House Conference on Aging suggested that the basic floor of income should be provided through a combination of payments from the Social Security system and payments from general tax revenues.[25]

Because income levels have bearing on all other aspects of a person's life—his housing, health, nutrition, transportation needs, and general well-being, the means of providing a guaranteed adequate income for the elderly have been the concern of many groups. One of these was the Senate Special Committee on Aging, which asked for some far-reaching and comprehensive reforms for meeting the retirement income problems faced by older Americans.[26] They reminded us that in this wealthy nation, nearly five million older persons live in poverty.

✿　✿　✿

Hilda Williams didn't need to read the statistics to know what was happening to incomes. As she often said to her closest friend, Mathilda, "Tillie, if Edmund had known that I was going to have to live like this, he would never have been able to rest peaceably in those final months of his life."

If Edmund had told her once, he had repeated a dozen thousand times more, the fact that he was happy he could leave her "comfortably off." Patting her hand, he smiled and said, "Hilda, I'm so glad we have this house paid off. My life insurance and the Social Security will keep you in good shape after I'm gone."

Hilda had always protested, pulling up the covers and busying herself straightening the bed, saying, "Ed, now, let's not hear any more of that. You're going to get well and go back to work, and that's that."

They both knew she was not telling the truth. Each of them saw Ed's pending death in the face of the other. Yet Hilda kept up the pretense and held on to Ed's assurance that she would have no financial troubles after he died.

For a time it seemed as if Ed was right. Hilda tried to adjust her life to being single. The little house brought comfort, and her garden gave her things to do. The children wrote regularly, and Hilda lived without too much pain.

But then school taxes went up, and property taxes were raised. The city approved a bond issue. Groceries seemed to get higher and higher. Hilda couldn't keep the car up and couldn't buy a new one. She sold it and then discovered that taxis were too much, too. She stopped going to the dentist and the physician regularly and then needed some expensive crowns on her teeth and some corrective surgery on her feet. The life insurance money melted, and the Social Security payments seemed to shrink.

Hilda began to think of taking in roomers or selling the house. She did not know where she would go. A gray depression began to settle in on her.

Decent Housing

People are like one another in their need for decent housing. Home for one family may be a two-story colonial brick on an acre of green lawn. For another, it is a compact apartment near the downtown area. Modest houses in small residential sections or farms miles from anywhere—any of these may be home.

For others, the place to stay may be a shack which offers minimal protection against heat or rain. There are those who pay for rooms which are always in twilight because no sun gets through the crevices between the tall buildings. Some are hidden away in roominghouses badly maintained and badly run. Still others are with relatives—unwanted guests who share a tiny room with a small child or who take up a needed corner of a living area.

Without decent housing a person is an alien. He has no "country," no place which uniquely is his own. His idea of self is diminished if there is not a corner which is his alone and where his treasures can stay with him. It has been said that home is where one feels safe to return. Without such a place a person is rootless.

For the elderly, decent housing where health and recreational needs can be available is an imperative. While many older people own their own homes, they often are drained by increasing high taxes and are unable to keep the houses in repair or to have them decently heated or cooled.

At the time of the White House Conference on Aging the Senate Special Committee on Aging reported that approximately six million aged Americans live in unsatisfactory quarters and that at least 120,000 federally assisted units needed to be built each year if there was to be hope of overcoming housing deficits.[27]

Transportation

Solitary confinement. Even the words strike terror in one's mind. An American officer who was kept as a prisoner of war for many months reported on his imprisonment by saying, "The most difficult experience of all was not the cold or the damp or the hunger. The worst was the solitary confinement, the having no one against whom to test my values or my ideas."

Mrs. Richards sits in the high-backed chair by the dinette window and looks out over the small Chinese garden. In her mind's eye she sees a small girl with hair of cornhusk silk racing her dog through a field. She can feel the breeze lifting her hair and skating across her skin. Her heart beats fast against the dotted-swiss dress. She senses the aliveness of the girl who moves with speed and with the spring sun on her face.

Mrs. Richards sighs, remembering. She would not move the calendar back those years. Yet she longs for that sense of movement. She is wistful with remembrance of rides in the country, sight of snow-touched pines; of walks in the city, new faces around her; of trips to other houses, old friends to visit.

Mrs. Richards stays immobile in her high-backed chair by the dinette window. But her mind takes flight from her large and lavish prison; only memory removes her from the solitary confinement to which her age has sentenced her.

Many older people in our society suffer the pain of solitary confinement because they are locked into their own homes or apartments or neighborhood and are unable to move outside the confinement of their area. Thus, transportation for the elderly becomes an important aspect of any consideration of needs.

Mrs. Richards living with her daughter in the suburbs may be as immobilized as Mrs. Wellington in a roominghouse in the city. If there is no decent transportation to take Mrs. Richards to a shopping center or a senior program (her daughter works and is gone all day), Mrs. Richards is confined within the walls of the attractive ranch-style home. Mrs. Wellington can barely make it from her bed to the kitchen and bathroom and back. To think of walking to the corner grocery is to dream an impossibility. Neither woman is able to be a participant in the life around her.

Some suggestions have included using schoolbuses and church vans plus all government passenger vehicles as transportation vehicles in "off use" hours and to make them available on a low or no cost basis for older people. Reduced fares on public transportation have been recommended and implemented, as well as special kinds of encouragement for volunteer drivers.

Without the ability to travel for medical help or job or for recreational or any other activities, the older individual is unable to be a participant in life. Most older people suffer from some age-caused immobility. Even if they are well-off, there comes a time when they should no longer drive their own cars.

For those who use public transportation, the fees are often too high, the scheduling or routes inconvenient, or the buses designed in such a way that old people cannot use them. For the rural elderly the problem is even greater.

Buses and subways pose the problems of doors which open

too quickly or need force in being opened or bus steps which are too steep for easy access. Crowding demands quick reaction time and strength in standing or pushing. Airplanes make still other demands. The long waiting lines, the necessity of carrying luggage, great distances between planes or between plane and exits all make for problems which are often beyond the strength or capacity of older people. Additionally, airplane cabins are pressurized to 8,000 feet, no matter how high the plane is flying. The slight decrease in oxygen carried in the blood at 8,000 feet may produce some difficulties among people with cerebral or cardiovascular problems.

Add to the above difficulties the fact that for many older people trips to the doctor for needed medical attention are expensive. The cost and difficulty of transportation may keep the elderly from seeking medical attention, even when the need is great.

The trunk of humanity which all men have in common may be covered by many branches which make people seem different—the color of skin, the state of finances, the nature of health needs. Similarities all but disappear behind such varied foliage.

We have seen that all people have likenesses. We all hunger and love and bleed. We all are needful of love, security, a sense of worth. We have sexual and health needs and desires for decent housing and transportation. We are alike . . . and we are very, very different.

CHAPTER THREE

Some Problems Among the Old—and Some Possibilities for Meeting Them

If life has been a matter of settling for too little for too long, if you have known second-class citizenship, if you have lived in a house that was ill-built and have eaten food which was not nourishing—what then can you expect in your older years but more of the same? For too many dark-skinned elderly in this country "more of the same" exists, only intensified by the extra difficulties of age and health crises.

PROBLEMS OF RACE AND POVERTY

Studies made preparatory to the White House Conference in 1971 reported that aged blacks are more than twice as likely to be poor as elderly whites. In fact, almost one half of all the older blacks are living below the poverty level index of $1,852 for a single person and $2,328 for a couple. That is only the average. Further findings indicate that almost one third of the elderly blacks had total annual incomes below $1,000. The black women living alone seem to be the largest group of poverty victims—almost eight out of every ten of them would be judged poor or near poor.[1]

With poverty come the ragged companions of poor housing and poorer health. Life expectancy is much lower for blacks than for whites. Although they do not use the medical services as frequently as whites do, they have more intense illnesses, resulting in significantly more bed-disability days than whites of similar ages.

Substandard housing provides minimum shelter for more than six out of ten elderly blacks. A high percentage of them live in the inner cities.

It has been postulated that people do not change essentially as they grow older but simply become more of what they already were. If so, the elderly blacks who have been discriminated against and who have spent their lives with inadequate incomes and unsatisfactory health services become poorer and more ill and increasingly inadequately housed as the years move on. The compounding of problems makes the difficulties of the aged minorities of urgent importance.

The fact that the "poor grow poorer" is proven among the aged. The older persons who suffer most from poverty are those who were able to earn the least and who lived the most denied lives throughout their years. While a fifth of the older families, about 1.5 million, had incomes of more than $10,000 in 1970 and about 2.5 percent had incomes of $25,000 or more, almost 7.2 million families with heads aged 65 or over had incomes of less than $5,053 per year and about 150,000 or two percent had incomes of less than $1,000 or about $20 per week. Another 750,000, or 10 percent of the older families had incomes of less than $2,000 and a total of more than 1.7 million or almost a quarter of all the older families had less than $3,000.

For older persons living alone or with nonrelatives, the income level was even less. Half of the 5.8 million in that category had incomes of less than $1,951; more than 700,000 (12.7 percent) had less than $1,000; and about 1.1 million

(19.2 percent) had between $1,000 and $1,500. A total of more than 80 percent of the older persons had less than $4,000 in income for the year.[2]

Although the numbers of families with heads aged 65 and over in the poverty level dropped slightly in 1970, the older black families demonstrated again the disproportion in income levels. For the blacks, 40.8 percent were living in poverty.

The black population totals about 22.7 million, but because of lower life expectancy, the black aged in 1970 came to 1.6 million, or only about 7.8 percent of all aged. For persons of Spanish American origin (Mexican, Puerto Rican, Cuban, Central or South American), the total number of persons was estimated at 9.2 million, while the aged made up only 3.3 percent. The American Indian population is estimated at 30,000 Indians aged 65 and over, about 5 percent of the total Indian population.

The compound problems of age and poverty and minority status make older years a constant hardship for many Americans.

If your name is Ethel Tompkins and you're black and poor and rather sickly, what happens to you when you're old may not be either peaceful or pleasant. Life has seldom been either, even when you were young and the fellows fought each other for the chance to twirl you around to music. There was always work. Mama lived in the servant's house behind the Lacys' big white brick, and you and Brother lived there with her and helped to weed the garden or pluck the chickens or polish the big trays of silver.

You played with the Lacy kids. When you were real little, you all ran races and jumped rope and shot marbles together. But they went to the pretty school down the street, and you took the old bus across town to your school. And as you grew older, the little spaces between you became a chasm. They left home to go to college and Europe and homes of their own, and you replaced Mama in the Lacy kitchen. When Mama couldn't work anymore, she went to live with Aunt Tillie, and you took over the servant's house for your own— yours and Harry's when you two were married.

There were your kids, just like you, with one exception. They left—as soon as they could get away. Harry left too. It began to get harder to get out of bed in the morning, and your back ached all the time. Mrs. Lacy's niece, who had taken over the house, got impatient with your slowness, and one morning she fired you—just like that.

And there you were, Ethel Tompkins, old, poor, black, with one paper suitcase of clothes and linens and a little metal trunk with pans and lamps and pictures and a couple of pillows you had cross-stitched yourself.

Where do you go now, Ethel Tompkins? You want to scribble a note to your daughter, Jane? Or if you're ashamed of your writing, who will pay for a phone call? What's Jane gonna do with an old mama when she and her husband have a bad enough time taking care of their kids? You think Marjorie wants you? She wants to forget you—didn't even write last Christmas. Marjorie's trying to better herself, and she can't get really better with you, old and simple, on her doorstep.

❁   ❁   ❁

Add to the problem suffered by the blacks another impediment of language, and it is easy to see that the elderly Mexican Americans find their problems intensified by the added barrier of lack of communication. The isolation suffered by many older people is multiplied when the old person cannot read or hear about programs or aids which are available to him.

To be old is one kind of problem. To be old and sickly is another. And to be old and ill and nonwhite is still a third. Add to those three the additional burden of being unable to speak English, and you find that becoming old is simply one more load piled onto the back of a person trying to make his way through the difficult field of life.

Information about numbers and ages of the Mexican Americans is often sparse. However, there are substantially fewer old Mexican Americans than are in other age groups. Life expectancy is only approximately 57 years; thus, many never qualify for Medicare. Because poor health is nothing new to them, and because the deductibles for hospitalization and physician services are often insurmountable, they are unable to seek preventive health care and often suffer from grave emergency illnesses.

Educational attainment levels are lower than for white age groups. Five out of eight older Mexican Americans would be considered functionally illiterate. The low education attainment is reflected in the lower-paid jobs which many Mexican Americans have been able to hold. In fact, nearly 63 percent of all the male Mexican Americans are blue-collar workers and another 8 percent are on farms. The aged Mexican Americans are considerably poorer than their white counterparts. "The median income of $3,756 falls below the $4,484 stated Bureau of Labor Statistics Budget for an older couple." [3]

The barriers to understanding services have kept many of them from knowing about Social Security, Medicare, and Old Age Assistance. The mobility of the workers has often made them unable to qualify for benefits under state residency requirements. In addition, many of them have worked in occupations which were not covered by Social Security. Those getting Social Security still receive very low benefits because of the level of their lifetime earnings. In general, they are inadequately housed, fed, and nursed. Others may have meager allowances from industrial accidents or the death of loved ones.

Take Manuel Rodriguez. You know him. He's the one with the straw hat pulled over his brown face. The chair he is sitting in looks as if it might crumble, but then the porch against which he is leaning seems even shakier. There is no grass in the yard—only packed dirt and rocks except for the small area where Manuel has tried to grow some vegetables. He can't keep the stray dogs out of the garden, and it's so hard for him to breathe that he can't chase them out either.

The landlord charges Manuel $60 for the one-room shack. It has plumbing with open pipes and a crumbling water heater. But Manuel doesn't complain. The landlord says someone else will pay more for the one room and little kitchen.

Where is a man to go? His wife—Rosita—died a long time ago and was buried in her green taffeta dress with a yellow artificial rose in front. The children—where are they? To other parts of town, to other towns, long gone. For a time Manuel left them, going to other towns to follow the crops or the building. Now they have left him. He does not know about the benefits for which he might apply. Most of the people in downtown offices speak English and have no patience for the brown-faced men whose tongue can say only the words in Spanish.

Manuel sits on the weak cane chair on the rocky land which is not even his. He eats only what he can afford to buy and has the strength to prepare. Long-ago delights of drinking tequila or making love with Rosita or lifting a log too heavy for other men—these have gone behind the heavy curtain of time, through which Manuel can see but dimly.

There are only the days which he counts off in Spanish and the tiny garden in the corner of the yard.

⋄   ⋄   ⋄

Other populations of deprived older people who are often ignored are the older Indians and Puerto Ricans. By any standards the elderly Indians comprise one of the most seriously deprived groups in this country.

Life expectancy for Indians is far below that of the total population because of all the negative factors which impinge on lives of Indians—bad housing, unsatisfactory nutrition, poor transportation systems, inadequate medical services. Unemployment among older Indians is extremely high, sometimes as much as 80 percent.

In a report of the Special Committee on Aging, United States Senate, the following was said about the elderly Indians:

Hunger or malnourishment is a way of life for most older Indians. Inadequate diets and limited information about proper eating habits are two major factors for this critical problem. And the impact of malnourishment is seen in many tragic ways for aged and aging Indians—a substantially shorter life expectancy, poorer health, and an inability to work in many instances.[4]

The report noted that bad transportation methods and poor roads kept the older Indian from being able to reach health care facilities. It also pointed out that present federal programs do not provide nutritional requirements for the needy, and an appalling number of the Indian homes are substandard with inadequate heating and often no electric power.

Summarizing the findings, the report added, "Much is left to be done, and no one can relax when the average age at death for the American Indian is 46 years." [5] The inadequacies suffered through a life of deprivation are intensified for the Indians.

Other populations who have often fallen into the "unwanted" category are the older Puerto Ricans and Cubans. Although statistics are sparse, the Census Bureau has estimated that there are almost 1.5 million Puerto Ricans living in the 50 states and the District of Columbia. About two-thirds of them are in New York City.

The elderly make up a small percentage of New York City Puerto Rican residents, and they are largely "younger" than elderly blacks or whites. As might be expected from the migratory habits and the poor educational opportunities which many Puerto Ricans have had, the income level is generally low, the median for a family of four being $3,811 compared with the New York City median of $6,091. Almost half of the elderly sampled have incomes under $1,500, and only slightly more than half of them receive Social Security benefits (compared with 70 percent of the black and 82 percent of the white elderly).

For the older Cubans (some 600,000 of whom have fled to the United States within a dozen years) life has been a matter of settling for low-paying jobs or welfare benefits. More than a quarter of a million Cuban immigrants live in Miami, and a larger number of them (about 6.3 percent) are older, compared with 3.3 for Mexican Americans and 10 percent for whites.

Again, the barriers of age and language keep many people from obtaining decently paying jobs. Poverty among Cubans is low compared with other minority groups but very high compared with Anglos.

PROBLEMS OF HEALTH AND CARE

Sufficient health and mental health care for the aging may be more dependent on public attitude than on placement of services. In a nation which spent more than $5 billion in 1970 on various cosmetics and hair-dyes and only $1.86 billion on Old Age Assistance, the negative regard for the older population is evident.[6] Only recently have medical specialties in gerontology been instituted. Real concern by teams of specialists for the particular problems of older people has been evidenced by a small minority of professional persons.

Older people, often passive, have often been ignored. In fact, one report states it thus:

What may be called a satisfactory "return to the community" may simply mean that the patient is no longer heard from. What passes for "preventive screening" could really be a de-

nial of any care at all. What may be hailed as new resources for treatment in the community may often be age-restricted.[7]

Health needs of older people too often have been denied by those who could render help. The fact that persons with reversible brain conditions are often turned away from state or general hospitals because they are thought to be senile and not ill has already been stated. More than that, "other serious emergencies are also refused admission. The chronic suicidal patient is denied care. Depressed, preoccupied, angry, and frightened, these older people take their own lives slowly over time. . . . No one is interested in them; they refuse help. . . ."[8]

Instead of needing less help in the mental health area, older people are likely to require more. Their loneliness, reduced financial state, and poor health may leave them with diminished self-image and purpose. Such mental states can then precipitate neuroses.

Mental Problems of Aging

Increasingly, experts are learning that mental illness in old people is not necessarily permanent. Much of it is organic, some is reversible, and some types are preventable. The fact that such illnesses have been regarded as unchangeable has often meant that the old person has been labeled without being helped.

Senility in old people still remains a major difficulty which needs to be dealt with in a helpful manner. Dr. Morton Leeds calls it the biggest single health problem facing our aging population today and describes it as a process of decline, some symptoms of which are forgetfulness, disorientation for time, place, and person, and return to early forms of coping with reality.[9]

The person suffering this condition demonstrates a great deal of anxiety, and often his judgment becomes so faulty that he makes serious errors. Family members as a rule try to ignore the symptoms until some crisis precipitates action. Then the older person is often placed in a state hospital. Dr. Leeds reports that many other kinds of community agencies can be called upon to help the senile older person, facilities which are more efficient and better able to meet the needs of such a person.

Senile psychosis comes about with actual atrophy or dying of the brain cells and usually follows a time of unusual physical and mental breakdown of old age. When the psychosis occurs, the patient begins to change his methods of personal living; he may become restless and sometimes violent. This person often makes serious errors of judgment and may develop new traits of delusions or paranoid tendencies.[10]

Although the majority of older people show a relatively mild decline in mental functioning in later years, organic brain syndrome does exist and needs to be recognized. A report put out by the Group for the Advancement of Psychiatry warns that many ailments may bear the symptoms of organic brain syndrome and must be checked out before any firm diagnosis is made.

The five signs of organic brain syndrome which should be present in some degree for such a diagnosis are:

1) impairment of orientation;
2) impairment of memory;
3) impairment of intellectual function;
4) impairment of judgment; and
5) lability and shallowness of affect.

The group emphasizes that it is important to get a correct diagnosis because some conditions, such as hypertension or brain tumors, can respond to specific therapies. Also, according to the report, patients who have organic brain syndrome have generally had pleasant pre-morbid personalities.

Because other ailments may mask as organic brain syndrome, true diagnosis and care can be difficult. For example, sometimes depressed patients may seem to have actual organic brain syndrome; so do those with hysterical personalities. Acute brain syndrome may occur because of illnesses like congestive heart failure, overmedication, or other conditions including fever and toxicity, liver disease, and others.[11]

The second most common mental disorder, according to Dr. Weinberg, is psychosis associated with cerebral arteriosclerosis, hardening of the blood vessels in the brain. When the vessels are damaged, there is a loss of mental function.[12]

However, an interesting finding regarding abilities of older people to function in spite of problems like those just mentioned is that the severity of the mental illness does not always reflect the amount of organic damage to the brain. In some instances, patients with much damage do not show much behavioral change, while others who have minimum injury may have complete dysfunction of behavior. In reporting on a group of volunteers, Dr. Weinberg said that many older persons who had severe psychological disease seemed to adjust to life and to live reasonably happy lives. They were able to live well with society and its demands and to make a useful and pleasant function for themselves within it.

Thus, while the actual damage to mental functioning cannot be ignored, experts demonstrate that much of the illness is far from irreversible. Our attitudes toward caring for the elderly need to be revised, according to persons who have studied older people. Many of the physical ailments are reversible or capable of being altered in positive fashion. A great number of the psychological and gross mental ailments are also manageable to some degree and in some instances can be reversed.

Institutional Care

Ask almost any old person what it is he really wants in his remaining years, and he will say that he wants to be able to take care of himself in his own home or apartment. Unfortunately, large numbers of elderly people in failing physical or mental health are forced to go to institutions. The phenomenon of the nursing home is an increasing one, and the numbers of old people entering such facilities have made the nursing homes a major "industry" in our culture.

In a study of nursing home facilities by a task force gathered by Ralph Nader it is pointed out that almost one million elderly people are in nursing homes, some 24,000 throughout the country. This number constitutes only 5 percent of the old people and the other 95 percent are charged with finding whatever care they can. Programs for home assistance are very few and often inadequate; so are intermediate forms of care for old people with special health needs.[13]

The study brought out the fact that many older people cannot afford the care they need. The deductibles under Medicare and the gaps in the program leave many old people with bills they cannot afford to pay.

Nursing Homes

For the more than 900,000 persons in nursing homes, care ranges from excellent to negligible. Standards for nursing homes have not been enforced consistently, and the dramatic tragedies like the 1970 fire in an Ohio nursing home which took the lives of 32 persons or the salmonella poisoning episode in Maryland, killing 25 persons, bring about outcries and investigations. Such studies generally show the lack of a national policy concerning institutional care for the ill elderly, along with the diffusion of services through numerous governmental and state agencies.

A preliminary report from the Subcommittee on Long-Term Care of the U.S. Senate Committee on Aging pointed out the five major causes of substandard nursing homes:

1) *a lack of a clear national policy with regard to the infirm elderly;*
2) *a system of long-term care with inherent or built-in financial incentives in favor of poor care;*
3) *the absence of the physician from the nursing home set-*

ting and in general the deemphasis on geriatrics in American medicine;

4) reliance on untrained or inadequate nursing staff; and

5) lack of enforcement of existing standards.[14]

First, fragmentation of laws concerning care of the old and infirm keeps a strong central frame of organization from going into effect on behalf of the older population. There are almost no options to long-term care other than nursing homes. Very little housing exists for older people, and auxiliary aid for persons living in their own homes is often nonexistent.

As for the second problem, the built-in disparities create some of the difficulties. Society's goal should be to return those people who can function somehow to their own homes. Yet some 77 percent of the nursing homes are institutions operating for profit. In order to make a profit, they need to keep their beds occupied. Also, ambulatory patients are compensated for at a lower rate than bedridden persons. The for-profit nursing home operator has less motivation to make patients ambulatory than to keep them in bed.

The third problem given in the report is seen in the few numbers of physicians in geriatric medicine. Medical schools themselves give little attention to the specialty, and many physicians find the discipline depressing and undesirable. Without a physician at hand in the nursing homes, the registered nurse (who often is busy with her supervisory duties) is mainly responsible for medical care. Her own schedule often means that such care is then relegated to the aides, who have little or no training.

The factor just named brings out dramatically the fourth problem stated, that of reliance on untrained or inadequate staff. The aides who serve in nursing homes are often totally untrained, and worse than that, disinterested in the plight of the infirm aged. One of the side effects of such lack of interest is the widespread use of tranquilizers to keep the patients sedated and bedfast. Some of the testimony given to the Subcommittee on Long-Term Care was that nurses and aides often were able to dispense medications on their own initiative. Other testimony showed that there were instances of only one nurse on duty for 130 or more patients.

Finally, then, the fifth problem, that of inadequate enforcement of standards, calls for careful concern. The relationship between federal and state offices makes for some of the difficulties. The federal government pays the major share of costs of nursing homes and gives out the minimum regulations, which then fall to the state to interpret. Because the states have for the most part been free to interpret the regulations and standards, the surveillance has been lax in too many instances. The Subcommittee documented instances of lack of enforcement. The state of Illinois admitted in committee hearings that 50 percent of its nursing homes did not meet minimum state standards.[15] Many other states in testimony admitted that they had closed very few nursing homes, although standards were lower than they should have been. The General Accounting Office for the states of Oklahoma, Michigan, and New York audited frequency of physician visits, fire safety, and nurse staffing provisions and found 50 percent of the nursing homes surveyed failed to meet minimum standards in these areas.[16] From other reports, these states are far from unique.

The five problems mentioned probably serve to key the many other areas of concern about nursing home care for the old. Citizens in every state have permitted such substandard conditions to exist because they were ignorant of the problem, or indifferent, or in some minimum cases, because they profited from them.

Operators of nursing homes do not have to account for the amounts they allot to patient care and the amount carried over for profit. Testimony given before the Subcommittee on Long-Term Care of the U.S. Senate Committee on Aging reported on insufficient heat, rationing of toilet paper, soap, and food—and profits of about 44 percent. One administrator admitted that he received $400,000 yearly from Medicaid, made a profit of $185,000, and spent 54 cents a day per patient for food, less than that spent by jails in the area.[17]

Time after time, investigations have shown many nursing homes which were negligent in providing safety standards for patients. Often where conditions were unsafe they were also unsanitary and hazardous.

Ask Mrs. Simmons. She is the one who came into the nursing home with a moderate case of diabetes. No one noticed or attended to the sore on her toe, even though her daughter called it to the attention of the nursing staff. By the time Alice's insistence had brought medical supervision, it was too late. Mrs. Simmons had to undergo amputation of her foot, and the shock has left her unknowing and unable to relate to other people.

You might want to talk to Mr. Ferguson, though he may not understand what you are saying. You had better ask his daughter, Hermine. Every time she has come to visit her father, she has found him lying on his bed in a pool of his own urine. The nurses always say that the accident just happened, though Hermine is noticing the bedsores and the raw places on Mr. Ferguson's legs.

Then there is Mrs. Alderson. Somehow her dentures were lost the day she entered the nursing home, and they have not been found or returned. Now she is suffering from malnutrition because it is almost impossible to eat the food without having teeth to chew it.

Mrs. Michaux smokes all the time, but she doesn't always remember when she lights a cigarette. Twice small fires have been put out in her bedclothes. But there is no guarantee that some night fire may not spread before anyone discovers it.

Or what about Leta Riley? Remember how she collapsed in her wheelchair one afternoon and almost died before anyone discovered that she had had a massive dose of the wrong medicine?

They say Mr. Miller would be able to stand and go around with crutches or a walker by now if the nursing home attendants hadn't kept him bedridden all the time without giving him therapy and the chance to strengthen his muscles. The stroke wasn't all that bad, and first reports had it that Mr. Miller might be able to return to his daughter's home in four or five months. He won't now, of course. He has been lying on his bed for so long that the chances of his being rehabilitated are pretty few. The worst of the matter is that Wilda, his daughter, really tried to get some therapy for her father. The nursing home executive promised to see to it, but somehow the program never came to life.

And so it goes. These are only a half dozen of the many thousands of old people who are placed in nursing homes from necessity or love or hope and who generally leave there only when they are released by death.

❊ ❊ ❊

Sometimes a nursing home can pose a double threat. The person entering the home is often filled with feelings of abandonment and desperation. But, when a mate is left "outside" while the spouse is admitted, there are special problems suffered by the "outsider," particularly if the partner has entered the nursing home for grave physical problems rather than because of severe mental confusion.

For example, the spouse who has been a part of the placement may go through a period of feeling both grief and guilt. "If only I had given better nursing care" or "if only I had prepared more nourishing meals" or "if only I had been home when the stroke occurred" may go through the mind of the remaining partner. The "if onlys" then become long fingers pointing at the spouse outside and turning all emotions into overwhelming guilt feelings.

When the "partner" suffers from disorientation, the "outsider" may again be guilt-ridden because of the complaints of mistreatment (often imagined) from the patient.

The partner may well undergo a real grief period, one as real and as devastating as that of the partner who loses a mate through death. Only, because this grief is striped with guilt it is more difficult to work through. The person goes through a period similar to that suffered by a parent who is confronted with the tragedy of having a retarded child, as described by Arthur Mandelbaum of the Menninger Foundation. In the instances of the parent and of the mate "outside," shame may well keep the person from discussing his own feelings.

Even stronger and more difficult to discuss is the death wish for the other person which such parents and such mates may feel. Perhaps neither group would react with so much guilt to the negative emotions if they recognized that aggressive wishes toward persons one loves are natural. As life savings melt, the resentment may also increase.

In addition to grief, guilt, and death wishes there is the nagging, non-clean feeling of small incidents unresolved, tiny quarrels hanging like a pollutant in the air. And there is, now, no way to blow them away.

Some of the services available to older people living alone are available to the grieving mate of the nursing home resident. Telephone reassurance programs can often be found by such a person living outside the institution. Friendly visiting can be sought; so can a program of meals. Counseling services are often at hand for persons who need to talk out some of their frightened and negative feelings.

The double-headed specter of the nursing home entrance, frightening to both the resident and the remaining spouse, may be shrunk by a careful recognition of this relatively new problem and by efforts to reach the "outsider" with positive programs of care.

❋　　❋　　❋

In a speech to the U.S. House of Representatives on August 3, 1970, Congressman David Pryor of Arkansas reported that we have turned over the sickest, most helpless, and most vulnerable patient group in the medical care system to the most loosely controlled and least responsible faction of that system.

Over and over, as medical and institutional care of old people is investigated, it becomes apparent that the care of the infirm elderly in this country is becoming a national crisis which calls for a concerted effort on the part of central agencies to set standards and enforce them.

Any examination of nursing homes also shows that there are many old people in the facilities who could be cared for in their own homes if there were sufficient extended care facilities to assist persons who are not able to care for themselves fully but at the same time could maintain independence if they had some auxiliary aid.

Although federal law requires that nursing home administrators be licensed, the owners are exempt from such requirements. Unfortunately for the patients, the owners are often removed from the nursing home operation. Many owners are corporations running chains of nursing homes. It has been suggested that one revision needed concerns the entrance contracts which require persons to turn over their possessions to the nursing home for life. Between 1967 and 1969 the number of nursing homes increased from 13,000 to over 23,000. The trend lessened by 1970 when government regulations regarding expenditures reduced the profits possible from the nursing home industry.

Some of the chains hold training programs for new administrators. However, the "trainers" do not generally have the experience to make the training really meaningful for those about to undertake the running of nursing homes.

✦ ✦ ✦

The job of nursing aides is one of the hardest and lowest-paid and yet perhaps one of the most vital to old people in nursing homes. The aides are charged with doing some of the most difficult tasks—keeping the patients clean, tending to their body functions, often feeding them, providing help, and generally giving the one constant bit of human contact which such old people may receive. However, in too many instances aides receive little or no training. The pay scale is so low that there are few monetary rewards, and work is so difficult and demanding that aide turnover is extremely high at all times.

Many aides begin the work out of a sense of devotion. Many of them sincerely want to help older people. They are appalled by the neglect they see; yet if their patient load is overwhelming and the satisfaction negligible, they too remove themselves from a scene which is depressing and ugly.

The old people themselves are helpless to report or protest or demonstrate. They lie, too many of them, in puddles of their own urine and feces, alone, neglected, and silent.

The quality of nursing in geriatrics has been upgraded in recent years. The American Nurses Association began in the early 1960s to give special attention to geriatric nursing. By 1970 there were 37,811 registered nurses who were members of the Geriatric Nursing Division of the American Nurses Association. The figures melt in consequence when one realizes that this number still represents fewer than two for each of the 24,000 nursing homes in this country, with no regard for hospitals, clinics, and special assignments. As stated, many of the registered nurses presently in such homes are involved in record keeping and administrative work, and the division of such nurses is far from even among the various homes.

Although physicians are supposed to be in attendance at nursing homes, they sometimes see patients only once or twice a month. Close surveillance of patient needs of medication is carried out infrequently in many instances. Often, when physicians do see patients on a monthly visit, the examination is cursory, sometimes taking no more than a few moments. This factor, that physicians see numerous patients on one brief visit, results in higher medical costs along with inadequate or indifferent services.

All of these professional lacks seem minor when one considers that the ingredient too often lacking in the nursing home is the one of concern and companionship. The volunteers who come so happily to pediatrics wards or who take amputees out in their wheelchairs are often reluctant to come into nursing homes "where everything is so smelly and depressing." As has been seen, the personnel themselves are often overworked and harried. Families of the patients are frequently unable to be in daily attendance, and the old people who are the "victims" are untended both bodily and emotionally.

To recover from any illness takes a great deal of emotional strength and determination. But to recover any of one's former competences in an atmosphere of neglect and human waste is nearly impossible. The old person who is in the inadequate nursing home because he can no longer take care of himself soon loses his will to live or to improve. Then, slowly descending the slide to death, he takes his tranquilizers and sits, quiet and unmoving, before the noisy mouth and eye of the television set.

The task force sent by Ralph Nader to inspect nursing homes recommended the following:

Stricter measures are in order, with contingency plans for caring for patients after cessation of payments to violators. The necessary expenditure for placing displaced patients in hospitals or specially licensed private homes will be more than compensated for if nursing homes are forced in the long run to offer acceptable levels of care.[18]

The recommendations also include ratings for nursing homes, medical review, training of aides, and alternatives for the elderly outside of nursing homes.

These findings are not condemnations of all nursing homes, of course. Many of them adhere to strict standards. Some are models of care and rehabilitation services. Many provide stimuli to activities and new interests. However, it is a sad fact that these progressive homes are in the minority.

Medicare benefits were set up to help provide decent care for older people. Along with Medicaid (welfare assistance payments), the programs were supposed to encompass the needs of infirm older people. However, in the study group report on nursing homes, it is said that of the 20 million persons 65 and over in the United States, 4.8 million are below the government poverty level and some two million more are too poor to afford the medical care they need. Out of these seven million people, only slightly more than two million were receiving Old Age Assistance by April 1970. It was also estimated by the Department of Health, Education, and Welfare that perhaps less than half of those eligible for Medicaid were registered for assistance. The deductible items provide severe handicaps for the aged. The report added that older people have less than half the income of younger people, but their medical expenses are nearly three times as great.[19]

Concern about providing good nursing home care increases. Herbert Shore has characterized the modern home thus:

A change has taken place in our thinking about the environment in which the aged live. . . . We have come to recognize that what was once considered "good enough" is currently being rejected by the present generation of aged. . . . Current trends and experience indicate that the future home will be a complex of specialized facilities offering a continuity and full spectrum of care.[20]

The "model" nursing homes look like resort hotels. The lobbies are plush; the grounds beautiful. Patios surround the living areas, and the colors of walls and draperies are rich and vibrant.

Reality therapy and remotivation processes are part of the

patient care in the best of the nursing homes. Everything is done to keep the resident oriented to the present. "Reality Boards," with slots for varied information, proclaim in every gathering room, "Today is ————. The weather is ————. The next meal is ————." Aides are trained to use methods to remotivate the persons in their charge, to try to evoke in them memories, observations, thoughts about any particular topic. Many efforts are made to shuttle the person back in time to memories of involvement and joys and concern and thus to try to help him retain some of those feelings and reactions in the present.

Two items which are lacking in many of the nursing homes, no matter what their financial status, are young people and meaningful involvement. An exception took place in one public housing project where a well-baby clinic was held on the first floor, alongside the recreation rooms and libraries maintained for the old people. The complaint of many old people had been, "We are tired of seeing other old people. We would like to see some youth, some children, some growing human beings."

The meaningful involvement is often bypassed in planning for the elderly patients in nursing homes. "What can we do *for* them?" is the question. Seldom is the query raised about what they can do for others. Although recreation programs are in evidence, few of them are mind-stimulants. Most of them closely resemble play therapy or game nights, but a minimum encompass classes, musical concerts, and discussions, projects which involve some of the mental skills which are latent. Even fewer deal with ways in which even the crippled nursing home resident can be of use to other populations of needy people or of service in community programs or involvements.

Older people in our culture have often been victims of what might be called a "Scarlett O'Hara Syndrome." The attitude of the public has been, "We'll think about the elderly tomorrow," and often in the planning of community facilities attention has been rooted in early childhood or in family relationships or in psychiatric illnesses per se without special regard to the older population.

State Hospitals

The senile wards of most state hospitals bear ugly evidence of the fact that many older people are placed in such hospital settings and then remain at the mercy of time and overworked staffs. Many of the elderly who have had psychotic episodes which were controlled or overcome have been "left" in the hospital by families who no longer wanted the responsibility or burden of caring for them. "Sometimes unwillingly, state hospitals have undertaken the responsibility for geriatric patients principally because of administrative policy. The needs of patients have tended to be a secondary consideration," according to Charles M. Gaitz and Paul E. Baer.[21] They consider the fact that state hospitals have often become dumping grounds for the old persons, even though other studies show that families do not place old people in such facilities as widely as they have been accused of doing.

Often the placement in the state hospital is not for reasons of senility per se. Frequently there are physical and social problems. The fact that no one facility gives comprehensive care for the geriatric patient means that many persons who are not mentally ill become residents of state hospitals. Conversely, numerous people who do have psychotic illnesses are in nursing homes.

The same problems which pertain to poor nursing homes apply to the state hospital facilities, with perhaps greater force. Wards are often overcrowded and poorly furnished. Recreational activities are few. Volunteers are almost nonexistent. Food is only fair. In other words, the atmosphere is often cheerless; so are the patients.

Take a walk into one of the hospitals and see for yourself. Do you notice the thin lady in the tall white rocker? She is sitting in front of the television set, but she is watching nothing. Look at her eyes and at her crossed hands. Nothing about her moves. The rocker does not rock; the eyes hardly blink; the hands remain tightly clasped. She is surrounded by other people, but she is alone.

Then there's Grandpa Spencer. He's the one in the overalls walking up and down the long hall. He shuffles some now, but he keeps on walking anyway, up and down as if he were going between rows of corn which he used to grow on that big farm he and Grandma Spencer had. It was after she died that the neighbors found Grandpa out in the fields at two in the morning, counting the ears of corn, and talking to Grandma, who had been in her grave three months already. The neighbors got worried and a little bit scared. After all, they had children to think of, and besides that, they couldn't be responsible for an old man living alone.

So Grandpa went to the state hospital. He brought his grief with him. He still talks to Grandma as he walks the imaginary rows of corn. But the doctors say he is not really mentally ill. He is shocked with grief and loss but could get better and learn to live if someone could be with him and help him walk from his phantom field into a place where there are people and laughter and youngsters with sun in their faces.

Or Mrs. Miller. She was staying with son Bill and his wife and had a nice little room and private bath. Mrs. Miller tried to help all she could too around the house and with the cooking. But Betty stopped her after she let the water burn in the pan of eggs, almost setting the house on fire. Then Bill saw her taking the wrong pills, and both of them yelled at her because she forgot to remove her nightgown before she put on her dress in the morning.

Everyone got very excited, and Mrs. Miller came to the hospital where she no longer had a room of her own and a private bath but was laid out, like an unknown body in a morgue, on one bed in a row stretching from the window almost to the wall across the way. Mrs. Miller is better now. She embroiders a little and watches the television. But Bill and Betty haven't offered to take her back home. They seem nervous about her being there with them, and there is no place else to go. Mrs. Miller will be glad when the good Lord takes her.

Drs. Gaitz and Baer report on a study of 100 patients aged 60–84 who were in a county psychiatric ward and were evaluated by a multidisciplinary team. They found that combinations of physical, cognitive, and social variables delineated the placements. They say,

The distinction between patients sent to nursing homes and those sent to the state hospitals points strongly to the extent to which physical impairments, in conjunction with the presence of organic brain syndrome, contribute to the disturbance. As is common for patients sent to the state hospital, the patients sent to nursing homes also appeared to have fewer resources available to them from the family and the community. The latter aspect appears to distinguish patients for whom long-term institutional care is provided.[22]

The study points out that the "healing forces of others" are not available in great enough numbers to help those people who are sent on a long-term basis to state hospitals or to nursing homes and who remain there on a lifetime basis. The proponents of varieties of long-term care would change that pattern.

In the work conducted by Dr. Gaitz and others, groups of patients put into local psychiatric hospitals were compared with those in state hospitals. As a group, the patients sent to the state hospital were more economically disadvantaged, as a rule had had previous commitments to the state hospital, and had not generally had their commitment petitioned by a spouse. While those who went to the state hospital were more disturbed than those who stayed in community facilities, it was notable that the state hospital patients had had very minimal community resources available to them. The "others" who might have helped with foster home placement or other kinds of intermediate help did not seem to be available to these particular patients. The same finding seemed to hold for many of the patients placed in nursing homes, who as a group seemed to have more needs for nursing care than did the state hospital group.[23]

Economic factors play major roles in determining who needs hospitalization and who does not. For instance, Mrs. Timberlake in her high-rise apartment overlooking the city bears little likeness to Eva Howard, the black lady who exists from one subsistence check to another. When Mrs. Timberlake is lightly confused, there is the ever-near housekeeper to talk with her, to give her a tranquilizer, to help her rest, or to bring her into reality. People drop in, too, and Mrs. Timberlake, with the help of caterers, is still able to entertain from time to time and go to concerts with her young friends.

For Eva the days are as dark as her skin. She exists in a small shack out in the country. Her neighbors sometimes forget she's there, and Eva herself forgets a lot of things. She doesn't always remember to eat, and on occasion she has wandered down the road and into the superhighway not too far from her house.

The two women, ironically, share the same birthdays in the same town. But there the resemblance ceases. Eva cannot remember how old she is. Not that it matters anyway. No one else seems to remember. The folks she used to know have all gone by now, and the boy she had and brought up alone is off somewhere and has forgotten he has a ma. Mrs. Timberlake knows when her birthday is. She is inundated with gifts, African violets, delicate pins, jersey robes, favorite chocolates. The passing of years is gentled by the care of physicians and the ministering of people who look to her comfort and her well-being.

Both women are old. This factor they share. But Eva has been hammered into thin, gray old age on the anvil of poverty, poor health, and discrimination, while Mrs. Timberlake has been cushioned by all of the appointments and attentions which money can buy.

Many of the aged, in this age of Aquarius, spend their time on a checkerboard of life, a square of day and a square of night. Days often are punctuated only by a period of grief or a dash of loneliness. Days of hopelessness are tinged with ennui.

However, even for the state hospital patients who are without resources, either financial or social, much can be done. The institutional walls need not close them against life activities, as examples of several therapeutic programs will show.

That the community concept can work, even for the aged, is demonstrated in programs which have been instituted in isolated instances and which are proving to be both workable and useful. Ypsilanti State Hospital can serve as one example.

Ypsilanti

Twelve hundred of Ypsilanti's patients are old, but two wards, designated as a "therapeutic community," are proving that the elderly mentally ill do not need to waste their days in graveyards of isolation. The expectation at the hospital is that the patient will return to the community and that he has not been "sentenced" to the hospital for life.

From the beginning, the community is brought into the hospital to become part of the rehabilitation team. Community agency representatives meet the patient and stand ready to serve as his link between hospital and community when he emerges from hospitalization.

The wards serving the older patients bear small resemblance to the usual "hospital white" barracks. Instead, colors bloom like flowers throughout the ward. Bedspreads are patterned; pictures decorate the walls; artificial flowers brighten corners. Clocks, calendars, and radios all help to bring the world of reality into the hospital setting. Patients are encouraged to decorate their own beds and chests with the treasures which have meaning for them. Staff members replace uniforms with street clothes, and doors are kept unlocked. Thus, the patients are welcomed into an atmosphere which resembles home and family more than it does hospital and "keepers."

From the first day when he is welcomed to the ward, the patient is taken on a tour of the facilities and is assured that he can participate in any which interest him. A self-government group helps people to relearn decisionmaking skills. Men and women work together and join in recreational activities. They sometimes shop in nearby communities and thus find their way without fear into the pattern of the larger world from which they came.

For the patients who seem to give promise of being able to maintain themselves in some measure, significant work is done before they are released from the hospital. Nutrition facts are reviewed, and the patients are taught or retaught some of the skills of living, from dialing telephones to using public transportation. The ones on medication are placed in a "domiciliary care" program where they order their prescriptions from the pharmacy and administer their own medications. Social workers take the patients to potential living sites, and the patients are able to react to the various possibilities as they talk with the hospital social worker.

Several research projects which have been undertaken concerning the milieu treatment program have showed its effectiveness. Almost half of the patients have been released from the pilot program, compared with one fourth from the traditional one. More of the patients from the milieu ward were able to live semi-independently, almost one fifth of them were able to live in apartments, while not one of the traditional patients could do so.[24]

The additional service provided by community persons to the Ypsilanti project is called Operation Friendship, geared to help the patient return to the community and to make an adjustment when he did so. Most of the patients selected for the program had been hospitalized at least a dozen years; a number of them had no family to whom to return; and all of them found the shock of responding to a changing environment difficult.

In Operation Friendship volunteers are trained by a staff of social workers. Club meetings and recreational activities are part of the package offered. Members make appointments for health care for the ex-patients; they help in finding living accommodations. So innovative were the plans that in 1966 the State Commission on Aging approved a 36-month demonstration project under the Older Americans Act.

Of the 79 patients who had been placed in the community, 72 remained. The facts become even more dramatic when one realizes that these were long-term hospitalized patients who, without the service provided, probably would have spent their remaining years on the state hospital ward.

Big Spring, Texas

Other hospital experiments have proved that elderly people, once assigned to a state hospital, do not have to be "sentenced for life." Imaginative efforts can bring some modicum of independence to persons who have been hospitalized even for a number of years.

For example, in Big Spring, Texas, an experiment with schizophrenic patients, many of them elderly, has proved rewarding. Chronic patients who had been hospitalized for many years and who were "filed away" in back wards were taken out of the ward setting and placed in protective living quarters on the hospital grounds. Technically discharged from the hospital, they continued to live in converted barracks nearby and to begin their work relationship by taking paying jobs in the hospital itself. The experiment proved so successful that some of the patients have been able to return to the community and to live independently; others have returned to the towns from which they came; still others have been able to maintain themselves in the semiprotection of the work village.

In addition, the rural area around the flat and sandy area of Big Spring, Texas, boasts Circuit Riders. The hospital itself, serving 48 counties covering an area of 2,000 miles, reaches out via its Circuit Riders, encompassing 120 volunteers. These volunteers who ride the "Circuit Wagon" work with elderly patients in the hospital and on their return to the community. They have contact with outpatients also and provide transportation for health or recreation activities. Circuit Rider referral offices and mental health clinics have evolved from the efforts.

One extraordinary result of the Circuit Riders project has been the help which has accrued to the volunteers themselves, many of whom are over seventy years of age. As reported by hospital staff observers, the volunteers have been helped to arrest possible mental deterioration in themselves because of their own involvement in helping other people. Thus, the circular effect of being helped by helping has beautiful reality in this imaginative program in West Texas.[25]

South Carolina

Even the once-considered-hopeless senile wards of state hospitals can be shored up and changed by the addition of persons who generate attitudes of hopefulness and cheerfulness. The psychological neglect of older people which has characterized much of the action of people in this culture has forced many older people to retreat into a cell of isolation where they neither reach out nor are reached by other human beings.

In one state hospital in South Carolina some years ago a back ward of psychotic senile aged was chosen for a study. Eighty-two patients were divided into two matched groups. The control ward, which was a little nicer to begin with, was left as it was. The study group was fixed up; volunteers were brought in; a milieu of caring was developed. Some of the women patients had not spoken in months or years. They lay

in beds side by side in crowded isolation, mute and incontinent. Sometimes they were tied into chairs.

Volunteers began coming into the ward, stopping to speak
to the women. Having learned about their past lives, the volunteers would refer to topics which had once interested the
women. They talked of daily life, of activities, of music, of
children. They paid attention to the women as people.

After a few months, results showed that the patients
placed in the study ward had improved both in social response and in appearance; those on the control ward had remained the same or had regressed. On the study ward one patient had died and one moved because of illness; on the
control ward five patients had died and four moved because
of critical illness.

Most dramatically, in the study ward women who had
been bedfast rose and dressed. One of them returned to the
piano. Others began to look at newspapers or to listen to the
radio.

The investigator summed up the results thus,

*Age is not a matter of birthdays but of functional capacity.
. . . The aging process itself is not our greatest problem.
Many of the difficulties that arise may be called social arti-
facts. They are often the products of misdirected human
workmanship, rather than the inexorable expressions of biological change. . . . All who work with older persons have
seen the recuperative powers many of them possess. . . . It is
axiomatic that what is reversible is also preventable. What is
needed most as a preventive factor for the problem of aging
is a positive change in social attitudes. . . .*[26]

Topeka, Kansas

Dr. Karl Menninger reported a similar experiment. Eighty-
eight senile psychotic patients at Topeka State Hospital were
selected. One had been hospitalized for 58 years; most had

been there for more than 10. A young doctor and "a thera-peutic team of cheerful young nurses, aides, social workers, and psychiatric residents" were assigned to the ward. These young people gave careful and individual attention to the patients. They instigated birthday parties and other activities. They played music, turned on the television sets, brought in pets to be noted. In other words, they gave full attention to turning the patients toward life instead of death.[27]

The results were dramatic. As reported by Dr. Menninger, at year's end only one of 88 patients was still bedfast and only six still incontinent. Twelve patients had left the hospital to go live with their families; six had moved out to live alone; four were in comfortable nursing homes; and only five had died. Out of the 88 "hopeless" patients, four returned to the community as self-supporting adults.

Dr. Menninger emphasizes the positive possibilities in treatment of older mentally ill and states that what seems to be "senility" may just be a temporary physical or emotional condition. Yet patients diagnosed as "senile" may often be placed in state hospitals where they have minimal care and where deterioration continues.

The experiments in South Carolina and in Topeka, Kansas, demonstrate the positive effects which can come about when older mental patients are given attention and assurance that they can improve and recover. The "therapy of friendliness" and concern can often reverse a "hopeless" condition.

Other Examples

In another state hospital, with a large population of senile patients, an alert therapist discovered that one woman who had tantrums and screamed angrily at everyone in her ward was quiet and helpful in the sewing room. The therapist decided that it might be good to put the woman into the sewing room to help make clothes for some of the children who desperately needed garments. The woman responded and was able to control her behavior as long as she was at the sewing machine and was able to function in a way in which she could feel her competence was being put to good use.

At another state hospital some of the women in the senile ward seldom received any gifts or cards from well wishers. They were enlisted to help make tray favors for patients in a tuberculosis hospital a few miles away. A visitor walking by one of the women one day stopped to admire one of the tray decorations. The old lady looked up, smiled, and said to the visitor, "Aren't they lucky to have us to do for them?" Conversely, of course, she was stating her own satisfaction and feeling of "luck" at having someone who needed her services.

In some nursing homes the simple addition of a work corner, where an old man can build a bird house for a child; a magnifying glass to help someone up in years relearn to discover the world; a weekly class where old people can teach some skill to needy youngsters or can read to or cuddle little children who are retarded or emotionally disturbed—any or all of these are being tried in order to see if the evening existence in any institution can be turned toward some sunlight hours. The public outcry over the plight of older people might well be lessened if the elderly are able to exist with a measure of hope and anticipatory pleasure.

Still one more example of how an indirect bit of attention can reach a hitherto unreachable patient can be demonstrated by an incident at the state hospital in Terrell, Texas. There on a psychotic senile ward was one old woman who responded to no one, would not keep her clothes on, and ate like an animal. She was a person whom the attendants avoided. She gave no indication that the human core of her being remained as she prowled animal-like around the ward, undressed and uncommunicative.

When a documentary film on Texas state hospitals was being made, the crew came to Terrell to shoot some footage on various wards. As is true in institutions, the word spread through all of the wards that photographers were going to do some filming there.

Where or how the word reached the "unreachable" patient no one knows. But for the three days that the film crew was in Terrell, she rose every morning, quietly and carefully, dressed herself and combed her thin white hair into a bun. Then she took her place unmoving in a straight chair by the window.

The fact that strange people might even inadvertently put her into a picture was enough of a stimulus to rouse the little old woman from her living coma and bring her own self from the blurred atmosphere of confused behavior and into the focused light of the living.

Perhaps the most serious problem of senility in older people and in their subsequent institutionalization lies not in the difficulty which the person is having but in the "eye of the beholder," the attitude of the society which lays judgment upon the older person who is having difficulty. Experiments like those demonstrated show the possibilities for reversal of senile trends in a large proportion of the elderly.

Discussions concerning institutionalization of the elderly in nursing homes, state hospitals, or community facilities must take into consideration the two-way bind in which many institutions find themselves. The Special Committee on Aging of the United States Senate reported the problem thus:

State mental hospitals . . . are ordered by economy-minded State legislatures to reduce "inappropriate institutionalization" of the elderly . . . but when attempting to "return the patients to the community," they are confronted with shortages, or nonexistence, of the very services that would make it possible for patients to make a successful adjustment.[28]

The Committee goes on to report that funding cutbacks have resulted in deteriorating care for patients in nursing homes and custodial institutions. Medicare discriminates against provision of mental health services for older Americans, and community mental health centers are not geared toward meeting the needs of the elderly. In addition, according to the findings reported, the pilot programs which have been successful in demonstrating what can be done have not been emulated or endorsed in ways which could be fashioned by others.

That the mental health needs of the elderly have been given low priority even by practitioners is stated clearly in the Committee report, which says that such practitioners are refusing to acknowledge that many ailments are indeed reversible. The report cites figures by the American Psychological Association that at least three million older persons need mental health services, but less than one fifth of them are able to have their needs met.

The Committee report then states:

In short, public policy in mental health care of the elderly is confused, riddled with contradictions and shortsighted limitations, and in need of intensive scrutiny geared to immediate and long-term action.[29]

The extreme need for public awareness of the condition of older people who also face mental disorder is stated by Committee members. They urge that concerned citizens take action to help provide care which can restore older persons to meaningful places in the community.

Some New Approaches

NORTH CAROLINA. In North Carolina joint cooperation among agencies has helped to provide useful care for mentally ill elderly. Many private and public agencies and resources have joined with the State Department of Public Welfare and the State Department of Health to give care for those needing it.

This coordination is carried out throughout the 100 counties of North Carolina by providing in-service training via state funds for persons working with the aged, by having specialists in aging in each of the counties, and by providing a variety of services, including mental health, to all of the persons in licensed group care facilities.

In addition to the multiple services given, many varied kinds of care are provided, from day treatment centers, night hospitals, centers for temporary treatment, screening programs, home nursing programs, and others. Also, many kinds of small group homes are found and help to give the released patients a family-like atmosphere in which to live.

PHILADELPHIA GERIATRIC CENTER. Not all mentally ill older persons need to be in institutions. As has been seen, a number of them can maintain themselves with provided protection in other kinds of living settings. In Philadelphia an innovative program has been instituted. Called the Philadelphia Geriatric Center, it encompasses in one city block a hospital, the Home for the Jewish Aged; two residential apartment buildings; the Gerontological Research Institute; and some small boarding facilities. Plans also include the Weiss Institute for the Mentally Impaired Aged and a day care center located elsewhere. Close to 900 elderly persons live in the facilities, which have registered nurses on duty and special services in the residential apartment buildings. Medical, psychiatric, and recreational services are available at the home and hospital to all of the residents without extra charge.

The multiplicity and coordination of services give a flexibility to the Philadelphia program which can mean care to the elderly mentally impaired at any stage of their lives.

MULTIDISCIPLINARY APPROACH. Coordination of services and of assessment must be instituted if the aged psychiatrically ill are to have the kind of care they need. A study undertaken in

Houston, Texas, demonstrated how hospital admissions could be reduced upon the instigation of thorough coordinated planning.

The study was conducted on 100 persons sixty years of age or older who were admitted consecutively to a county psychiatric screening ward. A team consisting of a psychiatrist, internist, social worker, nurse, and psychologist examined each elderly patient. A total exchange of information and plans about treatment was made among the team members, who decided together on the overall plan. Many existing community resources were brought into play to help the patient once he had been examined.

The complexity of the plan is described by the researchers as follows:

The purpose of the assessment will largely determine not only what should be assessed but also the manner and technique of assessment, and how it should be reported. A practitioner will find a number or percentile rating useful only if he understands its relationship to other capacities and other inferences.[30]

In this experiment the researchers appraised the total life situations and worked with all of the important "others" in developing the treatment plan for each person. A treatment plan was developed and implemented by a coordinator, and followup evaluations were made six and twelve months later.

Although there were a number of obstacles to the giving of care, efforts were made to achieve coordination and communication among professional persons and agency representatives.[31] Obstacles encountered included attributes of the patients, patient-family interactions, attributes of professional caregivers, adequacy of community resources and organizations, multidisciplinary interactions, and attributes of the case coordinator.

Finally, the study team tackled the problem of placement of psychiatric patients.

After all examinations were completed, the team members conferred and worked out a treatment plan. A control group of 110 patients who had not been initially evaluated by the team was selected for comparison. Of these 110, 79 had been placed in state hospitals. Of the study group, 22 patients were placed in noninstitutional settings, 24 in a local psychiatric hospital, 23 in a state psychiatric hospital, 23 in a nursing home, and 8 in a local general hospital.[32]

Thus, it can be seen that it is possible to decrease in numbers the patients placed in state hospitals. To do so, according to the researchers, would be to establish a network of psychogeriatric centers to give the entire comprehensive range of services. The paucity of resources available to the long-term nursing home patient serves to substantiate the fact that intensive and coordinated community efforts can help to restore many psychiatrically ill older persons to relatively functional places in the community instead of making them life-long candidates for institutional care. Commitment of community organizations and persons may aid in revitalizing coping functions for many older persons.

Some Recommendations

The committee specifically charged with looking at long-term care at the White House Conference on Aging in December 1971 made a number of recommendations. The first of these was that all long-term institutional care aspects of the Title XIX (Medicaid) program be completely federalized, with uniform minimum level of benefits. They also recommended that the possibility of transferring long-term institutional care aspects of the Medicare program to the Medicaid program be studied.

Nursing homes came in for their share of discussion by the people involved, and the recommendation was that the Department of Health, Education, and Welfare try to change the primary emphasis on nursing home inspections from physical plant standards to direct patient care.

The group continued with its deliberations and requested that there be implementation and financing of a national policy on long-term care and that physicians be encouraged to accept responsibility for the medical care of patients in long-term care facilities and that they be reimbursed at a reasonable established fee. The group also requested that more registered nurses be placed in leadership positions in all of the programs which involve health care of the elderly at governmental levels.[33]

The Group for the Advancement of Psychiatry, an organization of 300 well-known psychiatrists, focused attention and study on the unique problems of the elderly and the responsibility of community mental health centers toward those needs.[34] Concerned over the fact that positive programs needed to be instituted, the psychiatric group attempted to offer specific suggestions about how to improve community mental health services for the aged. They suggest the following procedure:

Every center should have an Advocate for the aged. Such a person will be the spokesman for the mental health needs of the aged within the center and also at times in negotiations with other agencies or governmental councils when such organizations make decisions that affect the mental health of the elderly.

It is especially important for some of the less sophisticated aged to be able to get mental health help without having to think of themselves as patients. A major way of accomplishing this is to give consultations to nonprofessionals who help the elderly with emotional problems.[35]

Some of the procedures recommended include staff education to help the staff itself in achieving positive views of aging. Another is clinical evaluation set up by an emergency home visit team. The importance of such visitation lies in the ability of the interviewer to glean information about the person in his own setting and to evaluate his needs. Outpatient services comprise a third recommendation, and the acceptance and welcome of the older age group in clinic settings are affirmed. Such procedures as group psychotherapy for the aged are recommended, as well as day hospitals. The fourth recommendation encompasses inpatient services, with constant work with the patient's family in order that they will not shut him out.

Frequent and available consultation services to persons manning homes for the aged, nursing homes, and to those people who are caregivers to the old are important adjuncts of any mental health program for the elderly, as are the ongoing assessing of needs and existing programs.

A social system model for working with older people is the primary design set out by the Committee, mainly because it deals with the person's ability to cope with his own life situation. In such a framework, the elderly are encouraged to learn leadership skills and to work on their own behalf; aid is given them at crucial points when such intervention is needed.

Continuing personality growth should be a primary goal in increasing the mental health of the aged, and healthy responses should be developed toward the changes which aging brings. The Group for the Advancement of Psychiatry points out that many of the elderly are not achieving the positive attributes of mental health, and they concern themselves with the overall social systems approach which encompasses all of the factors which impinge on the person. They state their philosophy thus:

A social systems approach to the prevention of mental illness and the fostering of mental health in the aged is as important as providing direct services to the mentally ill aged, because such basic requirements of mental health in old age as adequate income, medical care, protection from crime, the respect of other people, a role in society, and skills in the use of leisure time are all social, political, and economic factors not controllable by [the] mental health professional alone. Thus the center staff should use every opportunity to inform planners and policy-makers in other fields about their potential influence on the mental health of the aged.[36]

Staff members in mental health centers should ideally divide their time between working with the aged and with other age groups. In this way they have exposure to and understanding of the needs of people at various development levels of the life cycle. Often they discover that what they learn about the ability to cope with specific problems in one age group has significant carryover for another. Also, they are reminded constantly of the fact that there are not problems germane only to one period of life but that the continuum is apparent at every level.

The many patterns described in this chapter are only a portion of the tapestry which is being woven on behalf of older people. Many other models exist. Still others are in the making. What is significant is that multiple efforts from people at all age levels need to be directed toward making life meaningful and full of small delights for that portion of the population who have too often and for too long felt abandoned or without use.

·CHAPTER FOUR·

The Masking of Emotions

Emotions may masquerade in various fashion. Therapists have demonstrated the complexity of feelings, as well as the "impostor" role which many of them may take. In this chapter we shall look at some of the interactions between parents and children, particularly old parents and their aging children, and see how oftentimes the "carryover" of childish patterns of behavior may continue to influence the life-patterns of the elderly.

PSYCHOLOGICAL PROBLEMS

The magician comes on stage. An aura of mystery and excitement rises as he prepares his props and discusses what he is about to do. The audience watches closely, hoping to find the well-hidden seam which binds reality to fantasy. But there are lights, distractions, attention catchers on which the audience focuses. Then, in a flourish, the magician completes the trick, making the audience gasp with the realization that things were not all that they seemed.

On the stage, in the theater, the technique is delightful, absorbing, and intriguing. In life, the emotional "tricks" which people play on one another may instead be destructive. They are often no less hidden from public view; they may not be recognized at all. Yet the truth remains that "things are not

what they seem" even more often in the psychological interplay between people.

The emotional residue of early relationships may be a dye
which colors all of life. A girl who has been treated harshly by
her father may, in later life, repeat to him the early treatment
which she knew at his hands. And all of this may go on without any recognition of the subtle interplay of revenge.

Guilt may seem to be love in relationships of children with
their aging parents. Oversolicitude may well be punishment.
Mature love can give rise to guilt. And ill health often becomes a tool for the manipulation of others.

We shall look at some of the psychological hazards which
face the generations. We shall see some of the mutual manipulations which are used and then shall examine ways in which
relationships can be strengthened, as we look at some of the
"new" problems of this culture and some of the "old" ones
which continue to exist.

Most of the examples given are those of middle-class families facing dilemmas of relationships with older members.
The very factor of middle-class status often means that
choices are possible. Powerful emotions are present at all socioeconomic levels, but a family without financial resources
or middle-class "expectations" may have fewer options from
which to choose.

The psychological problems discussed have been divided
into three groups: those of control, reliance, and residuals.
However, no topic is "neat." Within each are mixtures of
guilt, anger, jealousy, resentment, and many "leftover" and
unresolved emotions from earlier years.

Control

The subtle ploys and manipulations which are enlisted in relationships between old parents and their offspring may wear
disguises of generosity, love, poor health, involvement, or any
number of other acceptable conditions. The "game" can be

played by either generation and with numerous variations on the theme.

Let's look at some of the ways in which control can be exercised:

Mrs. Richards has always been frail. Childbirth almost killed her, and Louis heard about it all his life. Besides that, she has had numerous ailments, from chronic sore throats to acute backaches, which have often kept her from attending parties, going on outings with the children, or entertaining guests.

Now that she is widowed and in her late seventies, she keeps the doctor's number handy by her bed, along with Louis's. Louis and Rochelle frequently entertain his out-of-town clients, and Mother just as frequently falls ill on the night of a party to which she is not invited. She calls, talking in so low a voice that Louis has to go to the study and close the door in order to hear her. Then she says, "Louis dear, I'm calling you only because I thought you would want me to do so. I fainted—or came close to doing so—a little while ago and barely made it to my big chair. My heart is racing pretty fast. I don't think this really means anything. I don't want to spoil your party, but I thought you'd be angry if I didn't let you know."

Louis listens, exasperation mingled with fear. Is she really ill, or is she just lonely? Is she being heroic in the face of serious pain, or is she trying to arouse his feelings of guilt over not inviting her to the party? He recalls the dozens of times his childhood had been disrupted by her emergencies, and he battles with the feelings built up over the years.

*   *   *

"Buying attention," even when it goes by the name of generosity, is another method of controlling others. It works like this:

Mrs. Perkins at 82 lives nicely. The resources left by her

husband keep her comfortable, and she is able to live in an attractive one-bedroom apartment with a small courtyard and convenient transportation.

She manages well, that is, on the outside. Inside she is hollow with loneliness. She has spent her years trying to mold life to her model, and those who were not bent by her manipulation have escaped her reach. Her husband grew more bent as the married years lengthened and escaped her bad temper only when he died—quietly and quickly—at a too-early age.

Nothing pleases Mrs. Perkins. If her daughter brings her a dress as a gift, the dress is the wrong color or cut or style. If her son takes her out to dinner, the food is unpalatable or the service deplorable. She spends her time in her children's homes criticizing their furniture or friends or methods of living. With her acquaintances she is also a one-woman argument waiting to land.

No wonder Mrs. Perkins spends much of her time alone. However, she knows that her young granddaughter and husband are struggling to make their budget work. She is aware of how seldom they can leave the baby and go out for an evening's pleasure.

Her method of operation is to call Sally on some particularly bleak day toward the end of the month, exclaiming over the fact that she has not seen her for many days. She hints that Sally will someday be receiving quite a "gift" from Grandma. Then she invites the two of them to dinner at the plush club down by the lake. Sally's hesitation is apparent, for dinner with Grandma means delicious food and constant attention. Grandma's insatiable need for praise and constant compliments gives even New York strip steak a taste of ash.

People viewing them out together at dinner may comment on the generosity of Mrs. Perkins, who takes the time to entertain her grandchildren. But she, who cannot earn their love, is in truth controlling them with her money.

✿   ✿   ✿

Some old relationships never die but are reincarnated. Sarah learned controlling methods from her father—and used them well!

Bill Henderson looked like a minister, even while still in seminary. Straight back, eyes like sapphires in the sun, a mouth that was firm and sometimes stern. Hilda, his wife, accepted her role and let William (few called him Bill) set the tone for home and friends. Quiet Hilda found her own self within the robust novels she bought surreptitiously in paperback.

It was Sarah who rebelled. She encompassed in her small-girl looks her mother's golden hair and clear brown eyes. Her emotions, however, were counterparts of her father's. No matter how stern Bill was in laying down rules, Sarah defied them. Whenever mandates were issued, Sarah bypassed them. When ladylike behavior was requested, Sarah dressed and behaved like a boy.

And so it went. By the time Sarah left for college out of state, Bill's hair had gone white and Hilda had retreated into a quiet death. The space between Sarah and her father widened.

And then it all returned. Bill's coordination began to falter, and a type of sclerosis was diagnosed. He could no longer fill the pulpit. Retirement benefits were negligible. There was only Sarah to whom he could turn.

Sarah took him in, and made a combination bedroom-study out of the spare room in her apartment. Bill planned to write a book, Sarah to continue her teaching of geography at the junior college.

But all the unopened feelings were like rotting eggs beneath the thin shell of congeniality. Conflicts, unresolved; angers, unspoken; furies not spent—these lay heavy as polluted air over the apartment.

Before long the old hostilities surfaced. Sarah reacted to her father as he had treated her as a child. She commanded patterns of behavior; insisted that he dress for breakfast; refused to take him to the barber's or the cleaner's when he wished to go. She became the stern parent-figure, and he was the recalcitrant child.

The feeling of righteousness which buoyed Sarah in her behavior melted into guilt when she returned from school to find her father sitting lonely in his room, silhouetted against the wall in the darkening shadows. She became gentle for a time, indulgent. Then some aspect of Bill's behavior pulled the trapdoor of memory, and she fell again into hostile relationship with him. . . .

*   *   *

When Grandmother or Grandfather comes to live with middle-aged children, the teenaged grandchildren may be the first and most intense reactors. Take a look at what occurred to the Blassingame family. Herb and June thought it only right to invite Herb's mother to live with them after his father died. They did not reckon with reactions of Shirley and Tim and their high school friends. They also did not reckon with the fact that Mrs. Blassingame had lost none of her authoritarian manner nor her need to control everything within her reach. Through the distance of years and miles Herb had forgotten that his mother had punished even a sick dog for throwing up on the rug and insisted that ivy grow exactly as she had placed it. With her children she was just as rigid; and now, in Herb's home, she immediately began to take over the "management" of Shirley and Tim.

"Never saw anything so undisciplined as those two," she said to June on every occasion. "What they need is——" and she proceeded to try to supply the supervision and lecturing which she felt they had missed.

June was trapped. Luncheons absorbed only an hour or so out of the day. The reading which she had enjoyed was now interrupted. Housework was supervised and criticized. The children grew resentful and began staying away from home with increasing frequency. The more they were gone the more Mrs. Blassingame criticized June and Herb for laxity.

Shirley and Tim no longer used the den for high school parties. Shirley talked in earnest about going away to college, out of state, after she graduated in June. Tim's anger and frustration began to come out in poor grades and poorer marks in behavior. He was suspended from school for being truant and acquired two speeding tickets, all in the first six months after Mrs. Blassingame started living with them.

Frantically Herb and June sought solutions. They quarreled over possibilities, and they rued their effusive statement to Mrs. Blassingame that "our home is yours."

Reliance

Reliance on others may be like a Ping-Pong ball. "Children" of any age can depend on their parents. Parents in their later years can rely on children for emotional satisfactions. Or, grown children and elderly parents can have dependent needs toward one another. Perhaps this kind of emotional reliance on members of another generation is the most deceptive of the psychological problems.

Some adults never shed their infantile interiors and thus cannot bear to permit their parents to reverse dependency roles with them. That was the case with Nancy Farabee and her mother. It was Mother who had typed Nancy's papers at college (and edited them beautifully while so doing). Mother took care of Nancy's clothes and needs, and Nancy smiled her dimpled smile and remained an adolescent.

Marriage did not change the situation. Nancy married close to home and stayed in the same neighborhood with her mother, who continued to bake for parties, sew clothes, sympathize with Nancy's plight, and remain a combination maid and confidante. She was capable with the children and the first one at hand when a child was sick.

Everyone had what he wanted from that situation until the years took over as taskmaster. Mother's hands knotted from arthritis, and her strength diminished. Nancy was intermittently worried, frustrated, angry, and guilt-ridden. But no matter which emotion was highest, Nancy felt a kind of grief, of having lost an important part of her being.

When Mrs. Farabee finally had to go to a nursing home, Nancy stayed at home and cried. Even on visitor's day, she had a hard time planning outings for her mother or special weekends at home. Somewhere back in the unconscious portion of her being was the hope that Mother would return, would be well, would be strong, would take over. And often that wish turned into anger, anger at the woman who dared to grow old and helpless, who dared to leave her, Nancy, completely on her own. . . .

*   *   *

In Thelma Epperson's home Mother had always been the showpiece. Pretty, Southern-born, Helen retained her soft accent and her pretense at helplessness even when her children were grown and she had been removed from Southern geography for years. Thelma's father, Mike, liked Helen as she was, enjoyed her dependency on him, and her little-girl ways. They made him feel strong, masculine, and assured. But Thelma and her brother Frank tolerated their mother with exasperation mixed with kindness.

And so life went until the day Mike died—suddenly—at the oil rig and Helen was left with the big house, many debts, and her little-girl mannerisms. Thelma and Harlan talked it over and decided that it might be good for Mother to have the children for company, and they would like having a babysitter on occasion. They invited Helen to come live with them in their ranch-style house in Oklahoma. The two children were young enough to double-up in one bedroom, and the sunny southwest room was prepared for Helen.

No one talked feelings to anyone else before the move. Frank told Thelma he would be glad to help with expenses, and of course Mother would be welcome to visit them from time to time. Thelma did not confide in Harlan some of her early resentments about a mother who depended on even small children to wait on her and do her pleasure. No one discussed with Helen what the problems were likely to be and how they might be lessened.

Helen arrived with her trunks of clothes and her own curtains and chintz chairs. Special shelves had to be built in the bathroom to hold her assortment of cosmetics, and Harlan made a swivel stand for the portable television in order that Helen could see her favorite programs whether she was lying in bed or sitting up.

Before long Thelma realized that she had a third child instead of a helper in the house. Helen could not bathe the children and put them to bed because of a rare rash on her hands, which also prevented her from helping with the dishes. Heavy work, such as changing her bed, triggered the bad disc in her back and cooking overfatigued her.

The sorrow over her father's death and sympathy she felt for her mother soon were overtaken by the Frankenstein monster of reality. Thelma recognized that her mother, with perhaps two decades of life left to her, had simply transferred her feminine dependence, which had served her well, into Thelma's home where it was no longer appropriate.

Thelma was caught between two poles. If she kept her mother in her home, relationships would deteriorate among them all, perhaps most importantly between Thelma and Harlan, who already were beginning to quarrel over items concerning Mother. The children had started to react to the tension, and Susie was wetting her bed again. On the other hand, if she "put Mother out," she faced the hostility and misunderstanding from Frank, from her friends, and from Mother herself. . . .

* * *

What seem to be the positive emotions of solicitude and concern may be covers for another emotion—anger. Arnold Cranfill did not know that until his ulcer gave him so much

trouble that his physician sent him to a therapist who de-
tected that most of Arnold's bad attacks occurred on Sunday
nights, after he had taken his aging mother out for Sunday
dinner and an afternoon ride. As he probed and attempted to
encourage Arnold to talk about his mother, it soon became
apparent that Arnold was filled with unexpressed anger at his
mother—anger which was not related to her behavior but to
the fact that she was old and that he could no longer rely on
her to sustain him emotionally.

In the discussions which followed, the therapist was able to
help Arnold see that he resented Mrs. Cranfill's inability to
walk well, her forgetfulness, her absorption with her physical
needs. Arnold, as an only son, had enjoyed a dependent relationship with his mother over the years. It was he who had
been able to turn to her when he was depressed or in need of
a loan, and it was Mrs. Cranfill who gave him not only money
but strength. She was dependable. And now, in a sense, she
had deserted him. She had moved away from the relationship
on which he had learned to count. She had grown old, and in
her aging she had become dependent. Now it was he who
needed to help her, both emotionally and financially.

Arnold Cranfill was angry—angry that he had been closed
out of a relationship which to him had had many satisfactions. But he could not admit anger, not even to himself. How
ridiculous to face the idea that he was angry at his mother for
becoming aged. How much more acceptable it was to express
his hostility in stomach pains and physical attacks.

None of this rationalization, of course, went on consciously
in Arnold's mind. It took a professional who could see the dy-
namics of what was happening to point out to him the delicate interplay of emotional and physical reactions.

Arnold's anger was interfaced with fear, the therapist indicated. Because Arnold and his mother had been close over
the years, the identification between the two of them was
strong. Each felt very much a part of the other. Thus, when

Mrs. Cranfill grew old and diminished in strength and competency, Arnold could see in her his own future aging.

In other words, Mrs. Cranfill mirrored Arnold twenty years hence. Arnold looked at her stooped back, her blue eyes clouded with cataracts, her trembling hands; and he saw himself, shrunken and diminished, almost erased from the blackboard of life. Arnold, who had always been proud of his abundant hair and straight figure and of his prowess with a tennis racket, could not face the idea that he, too, should be whittled by time. His mother was a reminder of his own aging process. He was afraid of what he saw and angry at her for making him view the future in an unpleasant fashion.

It took a number of sessions before Arnold could be helped to understand that in a youth culture like that of the United States it was indeed difficult to look upon aging as anything but a loss. He also had to learn that emotions could not be hidden without penalty and that what would not be faced openly would burrow in and return in another disguise.

As soon as Arnold was aware that his ulcer was his anger and his dependence in physical coating, he was then emotionally able to treat his mother with the usual solicitude and concern, but he also was able to meet himself and his future with more reality and forthrightness. In addition, Arnold faced still another reality. If he lived long enough, old age was inevitable for him. Instead of fighting it as he had been doing, he began to react positively by trying to learn some of the ways in which his older years could be made meaningful and satisfying.

Residuals

Old emotions—like old generals—never die; nor do they fade away. Instead they remain, buried and near-forgotten, only to rise again at unexpected times of life. Such feelings can come from jealousy experienced by siblings, from childhood resentments, from guilt, from parent-child rivalry, or from any

number of other emotional experiences. The fact is that unresolved emotional problems can appear forcefully and unex-
pectedly. They are most likely to make their presence felt at
a time of crisis when defenses are down. Let us see how they
can manifest themselves.

Sibling rivalry—denied, put away, almost forgotten—can
bubble up when an older parent needs special care. Millie
and Charlotte soon found out that the small-girl furies had
not dissipated in the air of time but had simply settled down,
unseen.

True, Charlotte with her two-year lead, had always had a
slight edge on boy friends, new clothes, and trips. But Millie
had outdone her in school grades (graduating only one year
later than she) and honors. Besides, Millie had almost taken
Jack away from Charlotte in college, and she had beaten her
in swimming meets. They had laughed about all the competi-
tion later on. However, the hidden rivalry continued, even
though they did not admit it.

It was Dad's death which brought all of the dark feelings
into the sunlight of scrutiny. At first, everyone rallied to
Mother's side. Charlotte and Millie and their husbands made
the funeral plans, talked with old friends, shared the tasks of
responding to sympathy expressions, and met the crisis in an
adult manner.

The souring began over Dad's will. Although the girls were
given equal amounts of stock in two insurance companies,
Millie complained that Charlotte's was more valuable. Then
when Mom decided to sell the house, the angry feelings were
uncontained. The massive dining room table—solid mahog-
any—went to Millie, who had the room for it. But Charlotte
fumed and insisted on the sterling tea service. Mom sat un-
caring in her room while the girls, in civilized tones, "discussed" the parceling of the furniture.

When Mom finally was unable to stay in the apartment
which had been her home after Dad's death, the old feelings
intensified. Charlotte and Millie, openly hostile, relived their

early conflicts as they battled over who "should" take Mom into her home. . . .

❁   ❁   ❁

For Martha Studer there was no question of keeping Mom in her home. She had fallen in the kitchen—living there alone after Martha had begged her to take a small apartment—and now the broken hip would keep her immobilized for months.

The nursing home only three miles from Martha's house was chosen for Mom, whom no one consulted. One day Mom was looking out the window of her hospital room admiring the crimson and yellow tulips below and the next she was in a nursing home with a cubicle of her own. "It's only for a little while," said Martha. "Just until you get strong."

Martha did everything for her mother. She refused to let her use the walker or dress herself. There was always Martha, every day, to keep Mom quiet and not let her exert herself. "What a devoted daughter," onlookers said. "How sweet," commented some of the visitors.

It was only a perceptive director of nursing who saw that Martha's oversolicitousness covered a guilt which she could not dare to look at in herself. From childhood Martha had resented the capacity which her mother had for making friends or bread or crocheted afghans. It was Mom whom people admired. Things were better when Martha went away to school and then met Dwight, who loved her without knowing who her mother was. But now, the old emotions, whale-sized, surfaced, and Martha could use the excuse of Mother's illness and age to keep her helpless and childlike in the nursing home.

The nursing director finally was able to help untangle the wire which had enmeshed both women. It was she who encouraged Mom to use the walker, to go to therapy classes, to take up knitting; and it was also she who found a foster home where Mom could live while convalescing. . . .

As seen in the case of Martha Studer who "took over" for her
mother, robbing the older woman of independence, decisionmaking, and feeling of worthwhileness, guilt disguised as
love can strike immobilizing blows, particularly at the older
person who is already feeling feeble or dependent. The child
who has harbored hostile feelings about a parent through
adult life may try to "make up" by overdoing for the parent
in later years. The one who has been heedless of parental
needs may, in a surge of guilt, try to do "everything" for a
mother or father who would cherish independence.

The young parent who disregards the emotional demands
of his children may try to compensate with toys and things
and food. The older "child" who has carried hidden angers
and hostilities may finally, in his guilt, overdo for the aging
parent.

The cycle, once started, can become a noose for both generations. Only a parent who has self-awareness and rare insights can honestly but lovingly disdain the extra attentions.
If the parent is himself needful and lonely, he will pretend,
even to himself, that the child is acting out of a sense of love
and is "devoted to a fault." And the rope tightens around
them both.

The hidden and dual negative feelings shared by parent
and child (at any age) may, unresolved, lead to increasingly
bad relationships not only between parent and offspring but,
with ripple effect, touch whole families. The mother who was
once beautiful and sought by men may ache with unnamed
longing when her daughter wins beauty prizes or is noted for
her own good looks.

It is impossible for the mother, even to herself, to speak of
jealousy and resentment toward a child. It is more acceptable
to herself to develop a crisis the day the daughter plans to go
to a dance or to become critical of the daughter's housekeeping prowess or style of mothering. Her need to diminish the

daughter's attraction results in her trying to make the daughter seem inferior in other skills.

None of this, of course, is overt or even recognized by either party. Rather, it reflects an immature method of handling emotions which are powerful and potentially destructive.

The same technique may work for the father whose son is growing into manly authority and who is beginning to take over in his life the roles which the father is having to relinquish. With the father, pride is often mixed with envy, and he uses his years of experience to downgrade efforts the son is making in his own business or social life.

Criticism which is billed as being "for your own good" is often criticism which is like a valve on a pressure cooker, releasing hostility in a hot steam of analysis disguised as helpful suggestions. The technique is just as workable in reverse. The son or daughter can use unjustified criticism as a method of making a parent feel guilty or hurt. If the parent gives a sizable gift to one child, the other offspring can respond with statements designed to be guilt-arousing in the parent.

SOME NEW DILEMMAS

A relatively new phenomenon is the situation of the "children" of retirement age who are still responsible for very old parents, persons who are often senile, nearly always semi-dependent, and frequently in poor health. Such a couple were Lewis and Letha Franks. His college teaching had provided a modest mode of life, and the two of them had saved diligently for retirement years. Lewis, an anthropologist, had for years expressed his dream to go to Israel and work on excavations there. Letha had read books and articles on the country to prepare herself for the year-long journey. The two of them had shared this dream even when the children were little and the savings money often went to the pediatrician.

Now, with the children grown and Lewis Jr. out of medical school, Lewis Sr. worked on his last semester of teaching.

They put their house on the market and planned for the new life, which they felt they had earned. That was the time that Lewis's mother, living with a long-time friend in Ohio, tumbled down the front steps, broke both legs, and was hospitalized. Lewis rushed to her side and finally had her transferred to the Missouri town in which he was teaching.

As painful day went into pain-filled week, as Mrs. Franks's mind became confused, Lewis was aware that, at 87, she might never walk again and might not be able to live with friends. What were they going to do? Letha and Lewis talked over the options. They could keep the house and bring his mother in to live with them. Of course, they would have to remodel the downstairs room and get some help for Letha in the long-time care of the invalid. Retirement funds would go pretty fast under such a set-up. Or, they could put Mother into a nursing home. The really good ones in town, they discovered, were expensive, far more expensive than the costs covered by Mrs. Franks's small pension or the help from Social Security or Medicare.

Even if they put Mother into the nursing home, could they go away from her for a year—or a month? She might be senile and often unaware, but the fact still remained that she was Lewis's mother. Would they feel guilty? Would their friends consider this a type of abandonment; and what would the children say? Letha and Lewis before long faced the reality that their dreamed-of excursion would never happen and that they would spend months or years of their "leisure" days in care and concern about the mother whose health and competencies had slipped outside the frame of her body.

They fought resentment; put down hostility; battled with guilt. Nevertheless, their angers came out in other ways, too often in terms of outbursts at one another. They recognized, as many couples in their sixties are beginning to do, that the "gift" of longer life has often laid a new task on the lives of persons in retirement years.

*   *   *

Parents in their forties may well be carrying the largest share of concerns, both financial and emotional, of any other age group. They are the ones who, having older parents, must plan for ways of giving them all of the aids they need. Conversely, they are also the ones who frequently have children in college and who must meet multiple financial and emotional demands of the younger generation.

Like the Indian, the "forty group" carries as papooses both generations, the one ahead of them and the one behind. In a culture of changing value systems and open rebellion by many youth, these parents frequently have the psychological dilemma of how to face the problems posed by the younger generation while still maintaining a poised and loving attitude toward the older.

The monetary demands are often of major dimensions. Parental needs for financial aid with living expenses or medication combined with youthful requirements for college expenses may overwhelm the middle-aged group of parents. The sometime difficulties of middle years, with their subtle disappointments in marriage or job, become enlarged as the husband and wife are pulled taut by the demands of both generations.

In previous cultures the years between 40 and 50 might be the "cooling periods" for brief old age. Most of the children were married or "on their own." Parents, if living, were in their own homes or part of extended households. Responsibilities of caring for both generations were beginning to diminish, and the couples in their mid-forties could begin to drop cares gently as a child would let toys fall from his sleeping hand. The new demands, the constant charge to produce, bring with them a pattern which is both tiring and frustrating to fulfill.

❊   ❊   ❊

Other patterns might be mentioned. There is the parent who has always been domineering and who refuses to let a son or daughter make decisions about his living or welfare. Such a person raises a dilemma for the child, who may see that solitary living is dangerous for the parent but who is reluctant to use force to change his residence.

At the same time that the long-hidden feelings of children toward their parents are being expressed, the emotions and needs of the parents are often at counterpoint with those of the children. The domineering parent in a daughter's home may try to run the household. He countermands instructions given to a maid by his working daughter, he demands obedience from the grandchildren, and he tries to command respect from everyone.

On the other hand, the needful mother living with her children may use every ploy at her command to win over the grandchildren by overindulgence or conspiracy about their behavior and may even extend her emotional demands to her children's friends and relatives. The struggle between parent and child (even when the "child" is past 50) may result in tensions in the younger family, withdrawal on the part of the older parent, and unhappiness all the way around.

❖   ❖   ❖

Much of the discussion has centered on parental relationships within their families. But not all people marry or have children; many older people know the tragedy of outliving their own children. What then of childless persons who grow old and needy?

The psychological hazards cannot be delineated so easily for this group, which may consist of childless couples or aging spinsters who make homes with sisters, brothers, cousins, or friends. Perhaps single men may live alone or with friends or family members. Sometimes brothers and sisters form a family group.

If the older persons are closely related, the same kinds of sibling rivalries described earlier may exist between them.

The subtle or harsh attitudes of parent-child may be carried out in older sister-brother patterns.

Without the often tempering effect of loving concern from a much younger close family member, the single older person faces the hazard of enlarging on his negative emotions and of dwelling on his hurts. Without the tugging of others to reach out or react or respond or love, a single person growing old may turn himself inward, contemplating his own hurts and angers and pains.

The childless couple are in danger also of hewing rigorously to old methods of response without learning the gentling quality of fresh looks at life or new ways of thinking.

These are the negative possibilities. They need not exist. Older people, whether single or married, childless or not, can find either penalty or reward in living. Much depends on whether they are able to give or receive what one psychiatrist calls "the healing forces of others." Whether they are able to look out the windows of their souls to see life take flight or whether they are absorbed in the darkness of their daily functions may indicate the manner in which their later years will be lived.

SOME POSITIVE POSSIBILITIES

We have seen patterns of relationships which turned bitter in the older years. One wonders if there must always be vestiges and "turnabouts" from stern parent-child relationship, as with Bill and Sarah; or dependency from mother to daughter (as Helen showed); or, counterwise, needs of an older daughter (like Nancy) to lean on her mother? Must buried guilt and hostility on the part of a child make her keep an older parent helpless, as Martha Studer did? Do childhood rivalries have to be renewed when older parents become dependent?

The examples posed so far are negative ones. However, the role reversals which children and their parents make are often carried out successfully. What are some of the ways in which needs of aging family members can be faced and various transitions made with minimum of emotional excesses and trauma? Are there ways in which aging within a family can be orderly, kindly, and meaningful?

One answer might relate to the response given about how one can be sure to be long-lived, which is, "Choose your ancestors carefully." In the instances of relationships in later years, the secrets lie in the seed of relationships from earliest years onward. Parents and children who have had open communication with one another, who have been able to bring anger and injustice into open discussion, and who have been honest in their responses throughout the years can often meet the trauma of crisis situations with a minimum of life-disruption. Relationships which were good are likely to remain good despite great difficulties.

Adjustment to old age may depend as much on expectation as on health or financial base. Sometimes persons who have been touched but lightly by modern technology and whose existence has been along the pattern of earlier years may find the transition from age to age as natural as the birth and death of animals on the farm.

Take the Williamsons, Marge and Dick. They still remain in the farmhouse which was Dick's father's and will be his son's (if he should want it later on). Dick resembles somewhat the live oak in the front yard—the one which is bent over, shaped by the weight of children in the branches over the years. Dick's face is furrowed like a miniature garden, and his hands are as rough as the rocks in the back pasture. Marge carries her years austerely, with a "no nonsense" step and a "right now" voice.

Both of them had worked hard ever since they married. Their children, all three, were born in the front bedroom. There were never any close neighbors and not a whole lot they wanted to do when the chores were finished and the supper dishes washed. They used to sit in the swing on the front porch and listen to the katydids or watch the sun go down. The radio, and later the television, kept them company.

The children grew restless, and all of them left just as soon as they had high school diplomas in hand. But Dick and Marge did not fret too much. They were used to the natural rotation of life, and they accepted what was to come with a simple faith.

Now, in their older years, they are as they have always been, only in diminished key and tempo. Dick still farms but only a small bit of garden, and Marge cans—but in pint jars instead of cases of quarts. The children write and come home some. Marge and Dick do not talk too much about what they will do when one is left alone or if they grow too helpless to stay on the farm. They figure that the good Lord, or the kids, or some neighbors—or maybe a combination—will look after them.

✿　✿　✿

Or look at Howard Kinsley, who, at 78, hopes he will have to turn to no one for help when he is finally beaten by the palsy which overtook him a dozen years ago. Neither the weakening effects of the ailment nor the bizarre shaking worry Howard too much. But the thought of helplessness or of mental deterioration keeps him open-eyed at night.

Courage is not new to Howard Kinsley. Orphaned when he was five, he spent the next ten years in institutions or foster homes, finally lying about his age and joining the Navy at the age of fifteen. It seemed that no one and no thing could like him.

Tillie tamed him some and made a home which was nice to live in. And the kids, Myrtle and Tom, gave him a lot of pleasure—along with plenty of worries. Howard progressed in the construction business, made enough money to send his kids to college, and even took a trip or two when Tillie insisted they ought to get away.

But now, with Tillie gone, Howard has put the house up

for sale. It doesn't mean much without her to keep it nice. What he plans to do is to buy a mobile home and see if he can maintain it himself for a while. He learns all he can about overhead supports and wall railings and hopes he will be able to get around.

Neither Myrtle and her husband nor Tom know how bad the palsy is. They don't see each other very often. Myrtle is in Germany while her husband finishes a tour of army duty, and Tom can't get away from his job up East very often.

Howard has taken himself around town to find out about costs of nursing home care. He figures his stocks and Social Security might add up to enough to keep him in one of those places, and he has decided to give his body to the medical school in Springdale.

So now he tries to shut out self-pity. He works as hard at that as he ever did on construction. He reads some, if his eyes let him, and he stays as active as he can. Howard's courage is special and unique.

❊   ❊   ❊

Howard Kinsley demonstrates that the parent and child who have been able to maintain a loving relationship which gives freedom to both parties are able, in later years, to have the courage to enlarge their own strengths and individuality.

As Erich Fromm has pointed out, "Infantile love follows the principle: 'I love because I am loved.' Immature love says: 'I love you because I need you.' Mature love says: 'I need you because I love you.' " [1] Dr. Fromm points out that the attitudes of mothers and fathers (as "ideal types") correspond to the child's own needs for the unconditional love given by the mother and the authority and guidance given by the father. Where the mother's attitude gives him security, the father's gives him capabilities to wrestle with problems.

The delicate problems begin to arise when the child starts to separate from the parents, especially from the mother. Dr. Fromm states that the mature person finally comes to the point where he is his own mother and father, or in other words, encompasses the motherly consciousness of unconditional love and the fatherly one of accepting consequences for actions. When the balance is not maintained, mature mental health cannot develop.

The ability or willingness for the mother to separate herself emotionally from the child has its likeness in the child who must break away from Mother. As Rollo May states,

Our needs are met without self-conscious effort on our part, as, biologically, in the early condition of nursing at Mother's breast. This is the "first freedom," the first "yes." But this first freedom always breaks down. . . . We experience our differences from and conflict with our environment. . . . This is the separation between self and world, the split between existence and essence.

Dr. May goes on to say that this first separation results in feelings of guilt. He points out that the human will always begins in a negative reaction, which is part of our wish also to redo the world in better fashion.

Willing in this sense [says Dr. May] always begins against something—which generally can be seen as specifically against the first union with mother. Small wonder that this is done with guilt and anxiety, as in the Garden of Eden, or with conflict, as in normal development.[2]

Since this sense of will which Dr. May describes must begin with "no," some parents interpret the reaction negatively and personally. Because of such parental reactions, the child may go back to the "yes" period, not opposing parental authority. The adult neurotics, says Dr. May, are those who endeavor to return to the perfect and nondemanding positive union with their mothers.

There are "children" of any age who manifest such neurotic dependence on parental figures. There are parents, even in older years, who themselves have failed to develop in mature and understanding fashion.

Such neurotic needs on the parts of both parents and children may evidence themselves in many hurtful and nonproductive ways as both generations face the needs engendered by the aging process.

Much of the adjustment to old age itself depends on the personality of the older person. The stresses encountered in aging have been compared to those of adolescence. Persons who have been able to work through adolescent difficulties and have grown into human beings who are for the most part self-accepting and other-loving are able to carry into their older years some humor about themselves and a sense of profound caring about other human beings.

The person who has been selfish and manipulative will, as has been shown, be even more selfish and controlling as he ages. Those who have needed attention throughout their lifetimes are likely to exaggerate their illnesses and demand attention for ailments of even minimum seriousness. Parents and children who have not resolved their mutual feelings of anger or hostility toward one another will "use" each other in destructive ways in the situations brought on by aging.

Some mature adult children endeavor to strengthen the competences of older parents, are willing to risk the worries attendant to letting the parent live alone, and encourage independence in decisionmaking. Through a mature love they may strive to keep the parent in control of his own life so long as he can function.

However, it is "outsiders" who raise the guilt feelings and destroy the pattern. "I saw your poor mother *walking* to the grocery store. She looked so feeble I was sure she wouldn't make it." "Where is your father tonight? You mean to tell me you let him eat all alone in his apartment?" "Your mother sat behind us at the picture show the other night. She was with

some other old lady, and they both seemed so lonely and bewildered."

No explanations then can change the overriding sense of
guilt.

Since no one can move back in time and change what has
already happened, the only options left are to practice basic
mental health principles for oneself and on behalf of the
other person. Perhaps one important first step is to recognize
the emotions for what they are. If childhood anger or feeling
of injustice or rivalry with a sibling can be recognized, if the
mummy-wrappings of long-ago emotions can be taken off,
then a person is ready to differentiate what is reality now and
what is overlay from unresolved sensations of earlier years.
Such revelation may be difficult to obtain, and sometimes it is
desirable that an outside person be consulted to help with the
sorting process and to suggest guidelines for behavior.

The psychological hazards which have been spelled out in
this chapter are avoidable for the most part if people can recognize them and can deal with feelings on an honest and
forthright basis.

One of the best techniques, as will be shown later, is to get
some physical and psychological distance between the persons most tied together in emotional problems. Both of them,
in each generation, need to move away from one another instead of clinging closer and tightening the raveling rope
which binds them.

Reaching out to others—strangers, persons who need
friendship and concern and the pleasure of conversation—is
one of the best ways of putting aside the personal feelings of
hurt, dislike, resentment, and guilt. With a stranger, one, in a
sense, starts clean. There are no buried angers, no unsettled
fights, no ugly rivalries which need to be settled and which
continue to lie, a scum upon the waters of one's life. Instead
there is the open and honest reaching of person to person in
friendliness and warmth. The ability to share with a contem-

porary some of the fears and delights of a particular age is
therapeutic.

The question at hand generally is not whether one or both
parents should move to the home of the children or even to
the community in which they live. The main problem is not
whether or not an ill older person should or should not be put
into a nursing home.

The real problem lies in the relationship of parents and
children and older people with others and in their way of
viewing life and mutual emotions. Guilt produces resentment
which leads to still more guilt.

The "uses" of people in unhealthy ways produce as large a
problem in this culture as the unproductive "uses" of goods
in the technological society in which we live.

CHAPTER FIVE

How the Individual Can Prepare

How does one prepare for growing older? For retirement? For possible single living after a lifetime of interrelationship with others? And when does this preparation start? The idea of retirement preparation in the cradle seems ludicrous; yet it has a certain amount of validity. The infant who is taught that all demands cannot be met instantly or who learns early to treasure independent action is already finding how, in the older years, he can use his judgment and ability in terms of useful action.

Just as we have seen that life is a single bridge arched across the river of time and not a series of pontoons, we know that old age and infancy are but opposite ends of the span.

Kahlil Gibran has put it thus:

And if this day is not a fulfillment of your needs and my love, then let it be a promise till another day.
Man's needs change, but not his love, nor his desire that his love should satisfy his needs.[1]

Each day is promise of another. The manner in which each day is lived becomes an indicator of tomorrow.

SOME MENTAL HEALTH PRINCIPLES

Man, then, is a sum total of what he has been and how he has looked ahead toward later years. The coping mechanisms he has learned, the satisfactions he has gleaned, the interests he has acquired all combine to make the later years useful or empty.

"Man is a product of his alternatives. The greater the number of alternatives, the better mental health he has and the better he can cope," says Dr. Ira Iscoe.[2] Not all of the alternatives are palatable. Some are unpleasant. Yet having the flexibility to face them and to make decisions based on them often helps the person at any age develop life-styles which will serve him well.

Having good mental health, then, does not mean holding the key to constant happiness. It simply reflects one's ability to squeeze the essence of joy from each experience, to meet difficulties philosophically, to face problems without being broken by them, and to endure discomfort without undue complaint.

Those who have been able to go through the stages of life, fulfilling each one before passing to the next, have been able to come to maturity without a backlog of immature hangups which keep them from functioning in adult fashion. The person who is able to go into his older years with emotional maturity is then able to cope with the new problems and crises which are products of the later years. He is able to be flexible about change and about the behavior and ideas of other people. He can listen to new ideas in creative fashion and can respond on the basis of his own experience and background. He does not have hidden angers or hostilities which need to be "played out" on other people in order to satisfy long-buried experiences in his own life. He is able to be open, recognizing his own weaknesses at the same time that he is aware of the strengths of others. He has humility without apology and self-esteem without arrogance.

Those who have practiced good mental health principles throughout life are generally able to adapt them to the special problems of growing older. For mental health is not in itself an entity but is only the ability of a human being to function with effectiveness and empathy within his life cycle. It is part of an overall life experience and is a reflection of thousands of experiences through the years.

Everyone is at times in an ebullient and sound mental state; at others he may be characterized as mentally ill. Often the evaluation depends on the degree of the person's reaction, as well as the duration of it. Any person who becomes angry and who loses control of himself is exhibiting a reaction which could be termed mental illness if that reaction continued for a prolonged period of time or if it were acted upon in some physically or socially undesirable way. The person undergoing a severe grief reaction is in a depression which could be characterized as a clinical "depressive state" if the death and grief did not make depression a "normal" reaction.

Goethe once said, "I have never heard of any crime which I might not have committed." Persons who read that statement are frequently shocked that a person of such creative and rich endowment could at the same time be a person who admitted to deeply criminal tendencies.

Yet Goethe was simply being truthful. All persons have destructive tendencies, the wish to kill or to mutilate others. What is significant, and what often characterizes the person who is mentally healthy from the one who is mentally ill, is how those destructive tendencies are acted upon.

Let's look at Buck Freeland and his wife, Lucy. Since Buck retired and Lucy gave up driving the car, they have been confined together in a too-small apartment. Daily they file away at each other's nerve endings. They know exactly how to do so. Lucy manages, every day, to pick up the morning paper before Buck has completed his reading of it, and to put the garbage in it. Buck leaves his "snack plates" on the drainboard without rinsing them.

Their frustration reached a point just short of violence when Lucy, rushing to the drainboard to pick up Buck's plate, tripped, fell, and sprained a wrist. Their perceptive daughter, Henrietta, persuaded them to go to a marriage counselor.

"Bunch of foolishness," growled Buck.

"What will he think of us?" moaned Lucy, "married 55 years and carrying on like children?"

Buck built a rack for his papers in the corner of the bedroom, and Lucy promised to stay away from it. They also worked out a system on the snack plates. But, more important, each of them learned how to handle the violent tendencies which would continue to arise as the two of them spent multiple daylight hours together. In addition to devising some activities which would be carried on separately, they learned how to "work off" some of their feelings. Buck volunteered to help the apartment manager keep up the yard and often swung an axe at some overhanging tree limbs when he was angry. Lucy took her feelings out on the pots and pans. After a particularly frustrating time, she was likely to scour every pan in the kitchen. By the time they were mirror-perfect, she was exhausted but no longer angry.

Seven criteria for characterizing the person with good mental health have been set out as follows by Dr. Henry A. Bowman:

1) On the one hand, he works for human betterment, but, on the other hand, accepts most people and situations, especially minor situations, as he finds them; he does not always expect everybody and everything to be adapted to his comfort and convenience.

2) He feels himself a part of a group, especially of society as a whole, and derives his satisfaction in life more through the contributions he makes to others than through selfish, self-centered gain or pleasure. He has an honest feeling of usefulness.

3) He is aware of his relation to the universe. He is interested in religious values. To some reasonable degree his life is oriented toward ultimate reality.

4) He has a reasonable amount of self-confidence. This does not mean overconfidence. But he knows his own abilities and limitations and therefore can meet life successfully. He is not steeped in self-pity. He does not feel the necessity of making alibis or altering facts to protect himself.

5) His personality is integrated. He is not torn by internal conflict—one part of him fighting against another part of him. He is characterized by a pattern of sound, consistent values. He is a whole person.

6) He approaches problems realistically and constructively. He does not evade problems and confuse his evasion with a solution. Nor does he try to solve problems through worry, nagging or complaint.

7) He has a very forward look. He looks to the future, not to the past. His life is not dull, or empty or boring because he has live and growing interests. He does not rest on the oars of previous achievement. He does not miss opportunities in the present by gloating over the "good old days." [3]

The principles laid out by Dr. Bowman could well serve as a guideline for future planning by those reaching the older years. The ability to approach problems realistically and to face the future with a kind of assurance is a characteristic which helps to give the years past 65 innovative meaning and character. Such a person, recognizing his own limitations, nevertheless works to the limits of his capacity for those principles in which he believes. And while he accepts himself with his failings and his strengths, he does not willingly accept injustice in the lives of others. He does not continue to cover today's life with the cloak of yesterday but instead takes today as it comes and looks toward tomorrow with a mixture of humor and of hope. The person with good mental health is able, ultimately, to live with himself—with meaning.

Mental health needs of older people parallel those of younger age groups; yet there are unique aspects which are depression-causing and which are often difficult to surmount. Dr. Jack Weinberg, speaking at an institute about aging, pointed out three types of suffering which are pertinent to aging:

1) *reality (death of family members, bad health, financial troubles);*
2) *civilization itself (isolation from a society which places its values on youth);*
3) *conflict between animal needs and moral attitudes of society (larger in the older person who fears losing mastery over himself).*[4]

Dr. Weinberg concluded that for the older people to obtain better mental health, reality would need to be altered as far as it was possible to do so. Where conditions cannot be changed, the individual can be aided in learning to adjust to the situation in which he lives. Societal attitudes, says Dr. Weinberg, are the responsibilities of all of us, while the personal and internal conflicts suffered by older people may need the services of a knowledgeable therapist.

SOME RETIREMENT PATTERNS

Reactions to retirement vary as greatly as do the individuals who go through the process. Depending on the state of their health, their life-styles, their finances, and their preparation, persons find retirement a new path to follow or a dead-end road.

People whose work has absorbed them totally may be like empty vessels when retirement comes. Persons who have devoted their energies to "keeping up" with the younger population may feel frustration, anger, and depression as they become aware that they can no longer maintain the looks or the pace of the young. Still others who have prepared carefully by marshaling interests and resources to take care of the older years can find later years meaningful and pleasant.

"Retirement may limit alternatives, especially in certain problems," says Dr. Ira Iscoe. "This does not happen if there has been preparation." [5] Dr. Iscoe continues that "anticipatory guidance" helps people cope with crises like retirement. For example, the first weeks after retirement may be accompanied by feelings of loneliness and helplessness. If a guidance counselor has told a retiree that such a period will occur, he can begin to master his emotions. Dr. Iscoe compares such guidance with the direction which a surgeon or anesthesiologist may give a patient contemplating surgery. If the medical professional tells the patient that a certain kind of pain will be present and will last for a specific period of time, the patient can marshal his resources to cope with the difficult period.

People meet retirement in various ways. They may plunge directly into new activities; they may retreat from the world. They may face the facts or ignore them. Some people pick up life where they are. Others go to different settings. Much depends on the person and the planning.

Let us look at some recent retirees:

Here is Tim Hefner. He had been with the automotive plant since the first year he was married. Being promoted to foreman had filled his dreams, and there was nothing he wanted more than to stay on the job and manage his crew. The kids were great, but he let Hilda take care of their needs. His wife was a fine woman too; her job was managing the home. He didn't have time for all the extra kinds of things other men did nor for picnics and socials.

Life was at the factory, and all the hours between were "tooling up" periods for getting back on the job. While Tim was managing his crew, his children grew up, grew away, had homes of their own. Hilda became quieter. Television replaced talk in the house, and Tim grew older.

One day it was July 11, and Tim was 65.

The company dinner was well planned. All of his crew and their wives were in attendance; so were the managers of the company. Hilda and the children were there too, all of them looking self-conscious and slightly strange. Tim wore his rented tux and made appropriate remarks about the gold watch and the pleasures of belonging to the company. Everyone drank champagne and then went home.

Tim was awake at 6:15 the next morning. Then it all hit him. He had nowhere to go and no reason for rising. He was retired. His life was over.

Tim spent the next week following Hilda around the house and complaining that he was useless and would be better off dead. At some times Hilda was inclined to agree with him. He went back to the factory to see his boys, but they seemed busy and not too eager for conversation. Besides, there was Mark, who had been promoted to foreman and who kept bragging about the amount of production the crew was planning to complete.

Long walks didn't do much good either. Tim didn't know where to go, and he thought about himself while he was strolling around the town. He felt like a fool in daylight going up and down the blocks and seeing housewives in their yards and kids playing ball—but no men.

Tim's depression had immobilized him before anyone thought to insist that he go to the mental health clinic and get some help with his problems. It took weeks of therapy before Tim began to learn that retirement plans should have started when he was a young man.

He also discovered that his reaction to his retirement was an all-too-common one, especially of men who had devoted themselves to business all of their adult lives. The "I'm not any good" syndrome was shared by many other persons and was simply one negative way of responding to forced inactivity.

Tim learned, in addition, that unless he involved himself in life, he was likely to have progressive depression and lowered mental faculties. He and Hilda finally worked together to pattern a mode of living which both of them found satisfying.

*   *   *

Maryalice Coltharp was not so fortunate. You wouldn't think retirement would be so bad for her, would you? After all, she still had her house and husband, all many women have in a lifetime. The fact that she had practically run the Harrison Tool Company and had seen it grow from a local firm to one of national substance ought to give her a lot of satisfaction. She had a nice retirement income too. What did she have to be blue about?

Maryalice wondered that too in the 4 A.M. blackness of the bedroom she and Joe shared. Joe still went to his office and took legal cases when he wished. But she was left to make the beds and scrape the pans and read aimlessly—she who for thirty years had managed to run an efficient household and an extra-efficient office simultaneously.

She was no candidate for the coffee klatch or the bridge group. She was depressed, very depressed. And she did not go to anyone for help.

*   *   *

Bartlett Miller was different. "No man really needs to be old," he was fond of saying. "I feel as good as I did in my twenties." Bartlett and his Ethel had been a part of the "beautiful young people" in his town, and they prided themselves on keeping their looks and vitality as they grew older.

Both of them began spending a lot more time at the hairdressers than they once had. Bartlett needed his sideburns "touched up" as they began to gray, and Ethel became blonder and curlier as the years went by. They entertained a lot and played tennis with the Carruths, twenty years their junior.

Bartlett never told Ethel what the doctor said after a checkup. He didn't believe that myth about "slowing down a bit" anyhow. It was a hot Sunday afternoon when the truth caught up with him. During the second set of tennis, Bartlett sensed the beginning of the chest pains which had bothered him for months. But he kept right on playing and was in the middle of a serve when he finally collapsed and was taken to the hospital.

The weeks of recovery gave Bart and Ethel a lot of time to think about the process of growing older. Both of them realized that words could not stop the aging process. Denial as a technique was useless and could be devastating. They *were* growing older. They could not hide the years, nor was there any real need to do so.

It took painful months of self-analysis to bring about the insights which helped the two of them to adjust to the role of older citizens in their community. They had to learn realistic self-appraisal, one of the most difficult lessons in life. But both Bart and Ethel were intelligent persons with many strengths. They were at last able to be honest with themselves and with one another. As they found out why they had had such a need to be young and why it had been so important to be well-regarded by their juniors, they then learned that they could harvest satisfactions from activities more appropriate to their own age group. Bart and Ethel were lucky. He lived long enough to find out how to age.

❖ ❖ ❖

Examples abound concerning ways of meeting the older years or the problems of retirement. No formula can be devised except on an individual basis. Let's look for a moment at William Hankerson, who seemed to step into retirement and a new mode of life with dignity and enthusiasm.

For one thing, Bill was a realist. He and Ann had gone through lots of hard times in their younger years and had often been "saved" from depression or collapse by a vivid sense of humor and an ability to look at themselves with some tolerance.

Bill and Ann knew that they were getting older and would, hopefully, continue to do so. Bill's eyes crinkled with laughter as he said, "I would be downhearted over getting older if I didn't think of the alternative!" Bill had become valuable as a management consultant and probably could have stayed on for a few more years if he had desired to do so. But he felt that there were certain advantages to retiring at the pinnacle, and he stepped down on his 65th birthday. No company dinner for him—and no gold watch! He cleaned out his desk over the weekend, except for some essentials. On the day of his retirement he finished a full day's work, gathered up the family pictures and his desk set, put them in his briefcase, and said goodnight to his coworkers.

Bill was awake at 6:30 the next morning. Unlike Tim he already had his day planned. He had promised Ann that he would build a greenhouse for all of the plants she loved to raise, and he started that first morning with his measurements and his lumber buying. Bill didn't let it go at that. Both he and Ann had for a long time been concerned about institutionalized retarded children in the buildings a mile or so away. They went to the first orientation program for volunteers and started on a regular basis to involve themselves with the retarded people on one of the wards. Soon the volunteers and the residents were in mutual anticipation of the visits, and Bill and Ann were able to enlist other friends of theirs into contributing time or money to help make life more meaningful for the young retardates.

❉   ❉   ❉

Retirement poses problems not only of personal activity but of the setting in which such activity will take place. Persons who have held on to family homes may decide to go to an apartment. Others feel that a warmer climate or a changed location may provide a better life-style. For some, the expenses of keeping up a homestead may become overwhelming; for others, the physical effort necessary to maintain such a setting may be too great. There are those who find the memory-packed rooms of a family homestead comforting; others discover that the convenience of an apartment has appeal.

Some persons left alone become afraid of solitary life and seek the satisfactions of apartment dwelling. Health needs may make others fearful of having no one around in case of illness or accident.

There are no pat answers to the vital question of whether persons should move or not. Instead the query has to be based on how important the security of home and neighbors may be or how adaptable the person or couple is to new surroundings, people, and modes of life.

Perhaps, as in most crises, decisions are better postponed than made hastily. The retirement itself, even if anticipated and planned, has certain shock elements. A gradual adjustment to the new life-style might be in order before any other plans are made concerning living arrangements. Such moves can be delight- or despair-producing, depending on the person.

Several new retirees may demonstrate how new living arrangements can affect people:

Warren Comstock decided to move. The day he retired he talked with the real estate agent about selling their home. He and Lila sat in the high-ceilinged living room before the mock fireplace and tried to place a value on the property which had housed them and their children for almost four decades.

If Lila seemed to hear echoes of children's laughter, if she saw evidence of the deep gash son Bill had put in the floor when he dragged his Christmas sled inside, if she could catch a faint odor of popcorn in the big kitchen, she gave no sign. She simply nodded as Warren and the agent talked about neighborhoods and square footage and possession and value. She kept telling herself that she and Warren had decided more than a year ago that they would move to Texas to be near Dorothy and her family, and the decision was good.

The excitement of packing and parties sustained Lila. It was only after they had moved and she found herself alone in the plain apartment one morning that the impact of the change struck her painfully. For while Warren still had golf and Lions Club, she was left with no ties except those to busy Dorothy and her equally busy husband and children. Lila had always made friends slowly and lastingly, and she could not imagine finding, at 64, some woman who could share her pleasures at bird watching or reading or quietly discussing the human condition.

Lila was lonely, with a desperate loneliness of an uprooted being. Dorothy tried, at first eagerly and later reluctantly and then angrily, to find suitable activities for Lila. The grandchildren were pleasant but preoccupied, and Lila wished herself back in the family home with the friends of many years.

o   o   o

The McDougals were different. Both of them, Beth and Harvey, had made friends easily. While Harvey was attending the testimonial retirement luncheon and receiving the traditional gold watch, Beth was packing the cut glass and the Meissen china and was chattering with her best friend, Hilda.

The trip to Florida, even with the U-Haul, wasn't bad. There were acquaintances with whom to stop every single night. And while the Florida prices were slightly appalling, Beth finally located a suitable third-floor apartment with a large living room and a bay window.

They found friends everywhere. In the beauty parlor Beth met a pleasant woman who loved to play bridge. Other people turned up in the neighborhood, at church, in the shops and restaurants. Both Harvey and Beth volunteered to help with the church Sunday suppers, and each of them joined in on the monthly church parties for a ward of mentally ill persons at a nearby hospital.

What the McDougals brought with them into their new life was their old enthusiasm and delight in people. They had spent most of their 37 years of married life entertaining company visitors and going to parties given by others. They liked movement and color and change, and they relished the opportunity to meet different people. The warmer climate of Florida was good for Harvey's increasing arthritis problem and for Beth's chronic bronchitis.

For people like the McDougals change can be challenge at any age. For the Comstocks and others like Lila Comstock any move can be a little death, taking from her what has been dear and cherished and enjoyed and replacing it with a feeling of emptiness and loss.

To move at all is a decision which should be made with thoughtful care. To move into a city where children live takes even more thought and honest weighing of plus and minus factors.

Tim, Maryalice, Bartlett, and Bill demonstrate some of the ways in which retirement and adjustments of aging are faced by various people. Variations of their responses and combinations of approaches are in use daily.

Some persons retreat. They start out by leaving everything familiar and take a prolonged trip around the world or around their state. If the trip is planned to keep them from facing the reality of life at home without a job, it is likely to be flat and unrewarding. If, on the other hand, it is a part of the fulfillment of a dream which the person or couple have had and for which they have made psychological preparation, it may be one of the finest experiences of their lives.

Some persons advance. They begin by pronouncing that retirement and the older years will be *full.* Then they boom ahead, like cereal shot out of guns, into frenzied activities which have more movement than meaning. They join groups; attend programs; start gardens; take apart the lawn mowers; enroll in gourmet cooking groups; begin projects that soon pall on them. By the time their energies flag and their enthusiasm diminishes, they are left with a dozen unfinished household projects, along with commitments to activities in which they have no interest.

Some persons stand still. They are immobilized. All of their lives their days have had shape and pattern. There have been the work days and the routine of making it to the office or the shop; there have been weekends with their tides of work and recreation. But now the waters are still, and they are halted, like moose paralyzed by dart guns. They neither retreat nor advance. They simply cannot move.

The factor of retirement is a growing one in this culture. Research findings concerning work and retirement raised the question of what implications widespread retirement holds for the use of leisure time and for the value placed by society upon the older person's new functions in retirement. The creation of a new class, the leisured older people, means that societal functions have to be regarded in fresh and innovative ways.

The importance of independence was stated thus in *The Older American*:

To most older Americans, a high degree of independence is almost as valuable as life itself. It is their touchstone for self-respect and dignity. It is the measure they use to decide their importance to others. And, it is their source of strength for helping those around them. Whether they enjoy the degree of independence they desire depends partly on the role they play in the community, partly on the condition of their health, and partly on the adequacy of their incomes, housing, medical care, and other essentials.[6]

The report points out that for many retired people nothing is quite so difficult or important as maintaining a useful and congenial place in the community around them.

For many retirees postretirement may resemble preadolescence. In the summertime, with school dismissed, the restless youngster wanders the house and yard and says to his companion, "Aw, what's there to do?" While the restlessness in the child is simply a part of growing up and is so regarded by adults, such aimlessness in the older person is an annoyance to others and misery to the person himself.

The "retirement shock" which many people seem to suffer can be reduced if active plans for the postretirement years are made long before they need to be implemented. Perhaps the word "retirement" itself needs to be changed, for persons, as they grow older, do not need to "retire from" life but to participate in it, actively, fully emotionally. Too often, as they take the word "retirement" literally, they leave not only their jobs but their social activities and friendships as well. When they do, they remove themselves physically and emotionally. Such removal leads to isolation, which is devastating to the human body, mind, and spirit. As the person becomes more and more isolated, he also becomes bitter and disillusioned, and soon the eroding circle of loss grows larger and wider and the person himself is lost within it. "A place" in the community, the family, and the self is an important adjunct of any retirement plans.

In recent years there has been a large rise in the number of people who retire before they are 65. Sometimes the early retirement is voluntary, and there are those who go on to second careers. At other times, the economy forces companies or military organizations to encourage and foster early retirement whenever possible.

Late retirement is most often seen in people who are self-employed. As a rule, they are most likely to keep on working until they are seventy or older. Also, those people who have few hobbies or outside interests are much more likely to continue with their work pattern than those who have exciting interests outside their careers. Other people postpone retirement because they have less than adequate income and are fearful that they cannot live decently without the salary which they earn.

Physical health may influence retirement. Those persons whose jobs require great physical expenditure of effort are most likely to retire for health reasons. Persons may be influenced to retire because their companies have set retirement policies or because Social Security or their own private pensions make retirement desirable.

The importance of preretirement counseling is increasingly recognized. Two-thirds of the country's largest companies offer some type of counseling to help employees prepare to retire. Many of these consist of financial rather than psychological aid. While the numbers of companies which have some kind of counseling seem large, only about 10 percent of American companies have intensive preretirement adjustment programs.

Many older people try out reduced work periods. Some work part time; others start small businesses. Others go in for leisure-time activity on a full-time basis. Some in the upper age group, if they can afford to do so, use the retirement years as time for travel. A study made in 1967 showed that seven million persons aged 65 or older took at least one trip in the preceding years and 56 percent of them took two or more trips. In contrast to those who travel, a number of older people report that watching television is their major occupation in retirement years.

Reactions to retirement vary according to a number of factors. However, in some instances, there may be parallels between being retired and having surgery or giving birth to a baby. Immediately after an operation or a birth there is a kind of euphoria, a feeling of having weathered a major event and emerged on the other side. It is only after a bit of time that pain or boredom or major concerns begin to impinge on the happy feelings.

For persons who have made some plans for retirement, the first weeks or months may be busy with chores left undone over the busy preceding years. One can see various newly retired people playing "catch-up" at their homes. One retired executive may be refinishing the antique desk he picked up some time back. Another is planting a vegetable garden in the back yard. Some women are in the kitchen baking; others have begun to do needlepoint. Many are cleaning up papers and straightening items in the home. Many more are taking off to fish or play golf or swim in nearby pools. In these first weeks retirement is like extended vacation, and the familiar comment is, "I've never been busier. I have more things to do than I have time."

But the boredom often seeps in slowly, a pollutant in the air of life. Papers finally get straight, as does the house. Baking becomes a bore. The tasks are completed, and fishing and golfing as a steady exercise grow tiresome. Then the downward spiral begins.

Many persons cannot face the idea of retirement, and for them depression sets in immediately. The day after the retirement ceremony there is a letdown which results in a depression which may be temporary or long-lasting. Generally, findings indicate that a person may initially be quite depressed but be able to rally until a period some ten years later when the negative feelings increase, perhaps induced by combinations of increasing age and poorer health, as well as lessening of contacts with other persons. Retirement itself has numerous major implications as far as the morale of older people is concerned.

A sage look at retirement is taken by T. V. Smith, who reflects that part of the problem is that "we lack a philosophy which makes old age respectable and which would prevent the normal process of decay and death from appearing as a surd in the life of reason." [7] Dr. Smith emphasizes that those retiring persons want not mere existence but the ability to go on living as people.

However, the specter of retirement is more often frightening than delightful. Even the persons who protest that all they want to do is fish or cook or lie in the sun and watch the clouds often secretly fear that their existence may crumble without the framework of job or career to hold them and to give them a sense of their own life space.

The Puritan ethic under which most people in this culture have been reared bears an influence on how people feel about their retirement. Our "guilt" at non-work is often expressed in our frantic following of various kinds of activities.

Other cultures see leisure in varied ways. Miss Santha Rama Rau of India participating in a roundtable discussion, put the problem in this manner:

I am wondering why leisure is a problem at all . . . I think it is rather sad that some kind of guilt has been built up in this particular society so that people feel that they should be productive in their spare time. . . . I think it is unfortunate that respect is gone for the man who simply sits in his rocking chair and thinks, if he happens to feel like it, or does nothing if he happens to feel like it. . . . So long as leisure is considered as a problem, it is certainly never going to be solved.[8]

FACING DEATH

What is life? Philosophers and poets through the years have asked that question. Scientists, working people, writers all have sought answers to the meaning of life. However, in recent years another question has become at least as germane.

What is death? And when? Is a person "living" when he is in a coma in the intensive care section of a hospital, with every body function performed artificially by machines monitored on screens? Is that life—or death? Does life end when the heart stops, or the brain? Modern technology and medicine have made it possible for a person to be kept breathing, heart pumping, for days, weeks, months, and even years. The fierce and swift efforts to meet emergencies with life-saving apparatus have meant that many people of all ages now exist like robots run by machinery.

The question of life or death now becomes one which is theological, medical, and psychological. Who has the "right" to turn off the machine, withhold the medication, or simply let the patient die for lack of attention?

Elisabeth Kubler-Ross, who has studied dying patients and has shared her findings in writing, feels that the current denial of the dying process and our camouflage of the dead have come about because death itself has become lonely and impersonal.[9] Dr. Kubler-Ross reflects on the dignity of persons who in earlier and rural cultures were able to die at home in their familiar surroundings and with people who loved them and whom they loved. The noise, lights, impersonal attitudes, and mechanical appliances which are attendant to the intensive care units; the tubes and needles and medication which are inserted and monitored; the "no visitors" sign on the door—all of these serve to keep the dying patient removed from life even before he is dead.

The disregard for the dying patient as a person with the human needs of every person for friendship and love and the warmth of contact is challenged by Dr. Kubler-Ross as the inhumane part of our care for the very ill patient. She states that attendants are so busy with tubes and other intensive care that they seldom have time to smile at the patient, to reassure him, and to regard his needs as a person.

The awareness that new attitudes toward the dying need to be developed is demonstrated in the practical as well as in the psychological literature. A front-page article in *Geriatric Care* stated, ". . . besides the strictly mechanical routines found in procedure manuals, it is necessary to enter into a direct relationship with the patient." [10] The article continues by saying that the patient needs more than someone to tend his body; he needs someone to talk with and to offer him comfort. The need for cooperation by all departments of a care facility—housekeeping, nursing, dietary, social services, and others—is stressed.

With understanding appreciation of the needs of the dying geriatric patient, the article also points out that when the patient asks if he is going to die, he may in subtle ways be really asking if he is going to suffer and if he is going to be abandoned.[11]

Those people who have worked with older patients affirm the fact that the elderly person has already faced the possibility of his own death. Most of them have suffered the loss of many significant others and have, in a sense, slowly died as the ones they cherish have gone from them.

It is often not the fear of death but the fear of dying alone or of being forgotten that tortures the dying patient. Psychologists have stated that one method of offering significant help to such a person is to talk about those qualities in the person which will be remembered and which will remain after he is gone. If there is family, reminiscences of shared and remembered experiences can help to let the patient know that his input into the lives of others will remain in their beings after he is gone. If the patient is alone, the nurse or aide can talk with the person about his qualities of cheerfulness or thoughtfulness about which others have commented. Often dying people are cheered by the idea that although they will die, their thoughts or feelings or good deeds will not be gone from the memories of others with whom they shared experiences.

Does death always mean defeat? Many physicians think not. One of them is Dr. William Poe, professor of community medicine at Duke University, who favors a new specialty called "marantology." The marantologists, according to Dr. Poe, would care for the hopeless old and would permit them to die without resorting to heroic measures to maintain a life process in people too battered to exist. Their physicians would not feel guilt when their patients quietly slipped away.

Says Dr. Poe, "Marantologists would not always look on death as an enemy but often as a friend." [12]

The idea that death is deeply dreaded by older persons and that thoughts of it occupy most of their waking moments is refuted in a study conducted by a gerontology researcher from the University of Southern California.[13] Using a sample of the aging residents in a retirement community in California, James T. Mathieu reported that his research showed that the subjects he studied had arrived at their fairly well-adjusted outlook on their own without the aid of institutional structures or society.

Only 4 percent of the 183 persons studied characterized themselves as being "very fearful" about the idea of death. Nearly 63 percent stated that they were "unworried."

The sample group seemed to carry out the general idea of most older people that in case of incurable illness, they did not want life prolonged. Almost two out of three of the persons interviewed stated that they hoped that treatments would be withheld and that medications would be stopped, except for those medicines which would help to relieve pain and to bring some comfort. Again, only 4 percent wanted "heroic" methods, all devices available, exerted on their behalf.

Refuting the practical and popular view that dying persons should not be told of their impending deaths, 8 out of 10 of the persons responding to the study stated that they would want their physicians to tell them if they were dying.

Discussion of death was no barrier as far as the older people were concerned, reported James Mathieu. Although the myth remains that the elderly do not want to speak about dying, the study showed that the persons interviewed were candid and willing to talk about the subject.

One surgeon at M. D. Anderson Hospital in Houston, Dr. John Stehlin, became so concerned at the disregard for the humanness of the terminal cancer patient that he worked with his interns in group sessions to try to help them in their reactions to the person with incurable cancer.[14] Dr. Stehlin reported that patients could respond in a positive manner to persons who acknowledged the gravity of their illness but still reacted to the personality housed in the ill flesh.

In a paper which he wrote about his work, Dr. Stehlin differentiates between the idea of incurability and of hopelessness. "A patient can tolerate knowing he is incurable; he cannot tolerate hopelessness." [15]

The wife of one patient who died of cancer reported that the greatest gift his physician gave him was not the medication and life-prolonging treatment but the recognition of the patient's intellectual interests. This knowledgeable physician spent much of his time talking ideas with the patient, debating concepts, and generally stimulating the patient with thoughts and possibilities. However, physicians as a rule are trained toward the saving or prolonging of human life and often are too rushed to respond to the patient's needs for conversation or reassurance. Auxiliary personnel, too, are likely to devote the major portion of their time to the patients who are curable and to regard the dying patient as no longer needing the services of quiet friendliness or cheerful reassurance. Dr. Kubler-Ross in her book observed that frequently she found the hospital staff desperately anxious to deny the existence of the terminally ill patient. However, while the staff might have been reluctant to observe the dying patient, the patients themselves responded favorably to Dr. Kubler-Ross's request for permission to visit with and interview them. Less than two percent of such patients refused to talk about their illnesses or feelings about dying.

The key finding from patient interviews is that concern with the patient's feelings and needs gives him a sense of communion with other people and helps to break the fierce loneliness which has gripped him during his illness.

Many persons who have been seriously ill and in a condition which kept them from being able to speak or to respond to others have reported that they were still able to hear what was said and to react to the spirit and tone of comments made. Examples of such instances abound.

One deals with a woman on the way to the delivery room to have a child. She motioned to her husband and asked that he have them stop the cart for just an instant as she experienced a gigantic contraction. The attendant merely looked at her and said, "It doesn't matter now. We'll keep moving."

A young woman who was recovering from a severe bout with mental illness reported on being in a catatonic state for many days. When asked if she could hear what was going on, she replied that she was able to know what was said and done from time to time, even though she could not respond to queries. The poignant fact she related was that one eager physician had brought a retinue of attendants in to see her lying in her unmoving state. He had lifted her eyelids, turned her hand, moved her legs and, without regarding her at all as a human being, said to his followers, "This is a perfect picture of catatonia." On the other hand, another physician found the time at noon each day to come to her and to press baby food between her lips, all the while talking with her of the day and its meaning and of life and its beauty. When she was able to react at all, it was to this compassionate physician that she could, finally, say some words.

An older man reported to friends that when he was returned from surgery and put into the intensive care room, he overheard one of the nurses saying to another, "Is he dying?" He tried with all his ability to move his head into a negative response in order to show that he was alive and intended to remain so.

Each of these persons in telling of his experience expressed his unhappiness at being treated as a "thing" rather than a person. Ill, almost unconscious, every one of them still clung to the attitude of being a part of the living. Each of them resented being relegated to the dead.

The full impact of what dying means in this culture has been stated vigorously by David Hendin, as follows:

Loved ones no longer slip away peacefully. Instead, when man goes, his mind is fogged by drugs, he is entubated, aerated, glucosed and comatose. He is alone, surrounded only, perhaps, by the hissing of life-sustaining oxygen. Surely the dying wonder why, after years of sharing sorrows and joys, they cannot be allowed to face the greatest of all crises with their family.[16]

Perhaps a parallel may be made with the present outlook on birth. Where prospective mothers were once drugged into unconsciousness and surrounded by strange and impersonal figures, they now are demanding the right to participate in the birth of a child and to be close to their husbands while doing so. If birth and death are life's greatest experiences, perhaps the parallel might be equalized. Dying persons, as well as mothers and the newly born, require the opportunity of being within the intimate area of their family life rather than being removed by geography and institutionalization to a sterile and alien environment.

It is to this isolation and lack of communication with other persons that Dr. Kubler-Ross writes. The need to talk with other persons and to share some of the feelings, fears, and anxieties engendered by the closeness to death is the greatest desire expressed. When those around the person deny him the right to face his own death with realism, they diminish the human quality in him.

Dr. Kubler-Ross tells of the "therapy of silence" which the dying patient needs in his final moments and expresses the hope that some one person who can understand that need will stay with the dying patient. She puts it this way,

Those who have the strength and the love to sit with a dying patient in the silence *that goes beyond words* will know that this moment is neither frightening nor painful, but a peaceful cessation of the functioning of the body. Watching a peaceful death of a human being reminds us of a falling star; one of the million lights in a vast sky that flares up for a brief moment only to disappear into the endless night forever.[17]

Many of the concerns expressed by older persons attending the White House Conference on Aging in 1971 dealt with death and with the rights of the dying to choose a mode and time of dying. The task force on Spiritual Well-Being had as one of its recommendations, "Religious bodies and government should affirm the right to, and reverence for, life and recognize the individual's right to die with dignity." [18]

In reporting on their task force sessions, the group stated that any discussion of spiritual well-being had to take into account all aspects of life, including those of death.

Many older people are asking not just for days of existence but for the ability to live and die in such a way that their fundamental qualities of humanity and of communion with other persons be maintained and that they be allowed to die as they have lived—with a sense of oneness with the world.

Often the difference between a crop harvested and one lost is the amount of frost which has hit. The same is true of older years. The psychological frost which strikes our older generation can be damaging. This need for love, self-importance, and emotional warmth is universal for people throughout the life-span. Aloneness is delightful when requested; devastating when imposed.

The individual can prepare for the later years by practicing good mental health principles, by preretirement planning, and by learning how to cope with crises. However, the person's own abilities need to "sun" in the warmth of concern and compassion of others if the "winter crop" is to be well harvested.

CHAPTER SIX

How the Challenge Might Be Met—Some Examples

If the aged in this society are to be helped to adequate lives in the future, planning must go on immediately at all levels. Present trends indicate that the elderly of the future will devote a much larger portion of their lives to retirement than do those of the present. The combination of earlier retirement and longer life-span may well mean that the typical older American of the year 2000 may spend a third to two-fifths of his life in retirement.

This booming number of older people with longer periods of life out of the work force presents a challenge to planners for the aging. Some of the projected figures which emerged from the preplanning of the White House Conference on Aging of 1971 showed that by the year 2000 there will likely be around 30 million persons aged 65 and over; a larger percentage than now exists will be in the upper range of 75 and older. If present trends hold, the ratio of women to men will increase; there will be more single older people. Also, rising costs and inflation may bring costs up as much as 50 percent, posing new problems for older people on fixed incomes.

The report states also that the aged persons of the year 2000 are likely to be better educated, have higher incomes,

and be in better health than today's retirees, more than half
of whom have never completed elementary school and one-
fourth of whom live in poverty, and almost 86 percent of
whom suffer some form of chronic condition.[1]

Is this new generation of old people a concern of the federal government? Of the states? Of cities? Religious groups?
Individuals? The answer to all of these queries is affirmative.
No one agency or group can undertake the amelioration of
needs of the aging population any more than it can take on
the question of education or pollution.

Aging concerns us all. How to maintain the basic human
necessities of adequate income and health while occupying
roles that are meaningful to society and satisfying to individuals is the problem which must be solved. Enlisted in the
problem-solving area are government, private industry, voluntary organizations, religious institutions, families, and older
individuals themselves. Many programs began as governmental experiments and were picked up by communities and implemented by individuals, often the older people themselves.
Most successful projects require the combination of federal,
state, local, and individual effort. Sometimes the local efforts
have evolved from governmental programs; at others, the national projects have been outgrowths of effective local demonstrations.

Tragically, some of the proven programs have disappeared
or diminished because of removal of financial support. That
human resources should be wasted or permitted to atrophy
seems incredible in a civilization which spends billions for
weapons of destruction.

This chapter will examine some of the projects which have
been attempted not only for the elderly who are poor and ill
but for those in good health and with adequate income. Examples of both public and private efforts will be described;
ways of locating experimental programs and other resources
will be stated; and some of the private efforts being made by
religious and other groups will be mentioned. Some of the

programs have been temporary demonstrations; others continue in existence. The examples are merely listings of what has been and can be done.

For too many older people life has descended to a pit of aloneness where waiting becomes the only activity of the days and nights. They are on a railway siding parallel to others, never crossing or touching. For them life becomes a pathetic struggle to exist when the meaning of existence is past.

"We are like travelers at a railroad station waiting for the train to come and take us away," said one old person describing what life was like for her. "All our goodbyes are said, and there is no one to wave to us as we leave. We are all alone, packed, and ready."

Many older people in one city were seen day after day in a huge bus terminal. On the straight wooden benches they sat, old women with worn purses and sweaters over their shoulders; old men hunched over their own knees, sometimes smoking on a long-cherished pipe. They did not speak to each other but sat as observers of a life in which they could no longer be participants.

Here the drama of living was being acted out before them. A mother wept on the shoulder of her son in uniform, while he embarrassedly patted her shoulder. A couple holding hands waited for a bus. In a quiet corner a mini-skirted girl with waist-long hair let the tears go unwiped as she clung to the tall young man beside her. A mother spanked a little boy; a child ran up and down in front of the benches, spilling peanuts as he went.

Mechanical voices boomed out the news that buses were leaving or arriving. People hurried; embraced; departed; returned.

There was life and movement, proof of existence.

The old people sat, wordless, and watched. It was as if they could be infused with life if they could be where living took place. And day after day they came by the dozens to spend hours on the straight hard benches and to try to take warmth from the fire of human existence lighting the dirty walls and floors of the bus terminal.

It is to put an end to much of the isolation which too many old people feel that numerous programs have been instituted. John B. Martin, former Commissioner of the Administration on Aging, has put it thus:

Five million older Americans live alone. Many of them are active, well, and continue to take part in community life. But hundreds of thousands of them—even those who are mobile and could participate—live in virtual isolation. The phone does not ring, there are no visitors, there are no invitations, there are no easy, affordable ways to secure transportation to a senior center, a civic program, or even to market. There are no incentives to action.

And for the frailest, the truly physically homebound, life is lived in a kind of solitary confinement destructive to mental and physical health and to humanity.

We have the tools to combat this dreadful isolation for older people. I am talking about programs which exist, at least in part, or could be created in every community. . . .

The result in human happiness and dignity will be worth it. Let's end isolation.[2]

Isolation can occur for a variety of reasons. Sometimes people are in fair health but have no money for services or recreational opportunities. Other persons are alienated from one another because transportation services are not available. Still others may live in rural areas and may not even be aware of the existence of some of the programs, if any.

Older people who live in cities away from their friends or family may often fall from sight. As the circle of their companions shrinks, they move more inside themselves and soon exist in the tiny compartment of their four walls.

Living inwardly, they often forget that they still have good to give and service to perform. They no longer think in terms of what they can render by way of help to other people. Instead, they are narrowed into the confines of the small area of life space they occupy. Yet it has been proved that many of these people can serve in a bountiful manner.

Numerous patterns have been tried. Still others are underway. Some of them utilize older persons as volunteers; others include them in paid categories. All of the programs attempt to give the older person meaning and force to his own life-pattern. In many of them the elderly are both donors and recipients.

As programs have been tested and proved to be successful, many of them have fallen into permanent slots with governmental or organizational agencies. Some of them have been combined with other programs under a single administration. Others maintain their semi-independent status.

Although sources of funding shifted after the beginning of 1973, nutrition programs on behalf of older people were considered priority efforts. Recognizing that nutritional efforts gave not only adequate food but also the opportunity for isolated people to meet together, the programs were continued in various ways and with a variety of funding sources.

NUTRITION PROGRAMS

Loneliness and good nutrition are incompatible, for eating symbolizes much more than food. The act of eating in our culture is an act of companionship where food and thoughts and laughter are shared.

Reminiscences about early life nearly always contain recollections of family suppers with the family gathered around the table; picnics in the country; snacks before the fireplace; holiday feasts shared by relatives.

Food is also a symbol of love. Psychiatrists have explained that the compulsive eater or smoker or gum chewer is subconsciously trying to regain the satisfactions he had as an infant suckling or as a child when he was pacified with food.

Food stands for comfort too. What small boy with a bloody

elbow has not picked himself up from a fall and run home, to be comforted by mother-love combined with cookies and milk? What grown man, staggering from some disappointment at work, has not been helped by a wife who prepared his favorite roast and hash brown potatoes as a sign of caring?

What then of the old person, stripped of companionship, diminished in strength and competence, who must eat alone day after lonely day? Earlier, we saw Mrs. Lester whose isolation kept her from eating properly. We looked at Mr. Smith whose diminished income will not buy necessary foods and at Gus Barrientos who did not know about nutrition and preparation of foods. We saw them alone and alienated and we recognized their hunger—for food, companionship, participation.

Many organizations working with the aged have recognized the need for food seasoned with laughter and meals accompanied by conversation. A variety of programs have been instituted; sometimes the older people themselves serve as volunteers, paid employees, or advisors.

Two factors seem vital to the institution of such a program. One is the provision of a setting which is accessible to older people. The other is transportation for those who cannot walk even the few blocks to where such meals might be provided. A variety of demonstrations have been started.

For example, in the commonwealth of Massachusetts, legislation has been passed to enable any school cafeteria or other nonprofit institution to serve lunches at a cost of 50 cents to persons over 59 years of age. In other areas school cafeterias have proved to be desirable sites for such programs.

A group of organizations has banded together in Denver, Colorado, to serve meals to an average of 700 older people each week. Five sites are utilized, with rent and utilities paid for by the Salvation Army, the Urban Renewal Center, and three churches. Serve A Meal to Seniors (SAMS) employs senior citizens, and the meals are prepared in small kitchens and served for 60 cents.

Commercial restaurants are cooperating also. One Florida cafeteria serves senior meals at special rates; a Los Angeles chain gives low prices and meals for seniors at nine locations; and a San Francisco restaurant offers a take-out package of three meals for $2.00.

In cases where groups are gathered for meals, it is possible to institute nutrition programs. Sometimes speakers give "luncheon lectures." In other areas, "potluck" meals are encouraged. When participants bring their own foods to share, there is also opportunity to discuss nutrition and food combination.

As these programs demonstrate the therapeutic effect of group eating, further efforts are being made to bring into the program persons who are handicapped. In some nursing homes weekly luncheons have been instituted, where nursing home patients can leave the sameness of their own rooms and floor and "go out to luncheon" on another floor or with a different combination of persons.

The Meals-on-Wheels program has become a well-known method of bringing good nutritional food to persons who are home-bound. Various combinations of methods are used in making these deliveries. In many instances where volunteers are used, it has been found that the volunteer's staying to visit during the meal helps the home-bound person in meal enjoyment and consumption.

In Baltimore, the program has expanded to the point that nine separate kitchens are used. Staffed almost entirely by volunteers, it was started by the Baltimore Section of the National Council of Jewish Women, aided by the Maryland Home Economics Association. Other groups joined, and a full-time coordinator was funded by the Administration on Aging. The "hidden agenda" of such a service is that the volunteers who deliver the meals can often report on other needs which the recipient may have.

Much more than food is delivered in a program such as this. Companionship is served on the food tray, friendship with a glass of milk. The symbol of caring which accompanies such a service is often as nourishing to the older person as the food itself.

Ask Mr. Wilmont. In his garage apartment he was pretty much a prisoner. He didn't dare risk the stairs by himself, now that he was on crutches; and there wasn't another place he could move to on his little pension. His life was bounded by a dirty alley at the back and the tall brick apartment house wall from his living-bedroom. No flowers grew on the asphalt parking lot, and no birds paused within his sight. There were just Mr. Wilmont and the impersonal television set. But when Meals-on-Wheels found Mr. Wilmont, Mr. Wilmont found a new way of life. With that nice Mrs. Freedman stopping in every day, he began to get himself cleaned up a little, and the apartment too. He also started listening to the news in order to have something to say to her when she came. Life was different, in a good way.

Or look at Mrs. Myerson. When was the last time she had eaten a hot meal or visited with people? She couldn't remember. Marilyn was so far away, and the grandchildren were strangers. So was everyone else it seemed. When the group meals were begun at the little school a block from her house, Mrs. Myerson was invited to participate. She went, at first reluctantly, then eagerly. She found that the walk made her feel younger and hungrier, and the companionship gave her a whole new look at herself and the people she met. Pretty soon she was a volunteer helping with the lunches.

Numerous nutritional-aide programs have been undertaken in various communities in every state. An interesting example of an effort to reach out-of-the-way older poverty people is "Country Gathering," a nutrition demonstration project which was funded from June 1968 through June 1972. Partially sponsored by the Department of Health, Education, and Welfare and the Office of Economic Opportunity and the Northeast Kentucky Area Development Council, it consisted of seven centers operating in six counties and serving 2,136 square miles of Appalachia. Older people staffed the centers and provided transportation to the aged participants to and from the centers. Volunteer retired teachers and staff assistants taught consumer education, nutrition education, and menu and recipe planning.

Group dining and activities programs for persons over 60 and home-delivered meals for the aged were maintained in Buffalo, New York, by the Council of Churches, Catholic Charities, and United Jewish Federation. Here federal and county funds helped to promote a program in which persons contributed according to their means.

In California, at the request of the Public Welfare Department, the Sacramento Red Cross Chapter recruited volunteers to secure proxies from eligible recipients of food stamps.

A service provided in Syracuse, New York, has maintained itself since its small beginning in 1960. Many sponsors have been enlisted. The Council on Aging, Midtown Hospital Board, Syracuse Housing Authority, and about 100 volunteers a week make this program successful. Only a part-time director and a part-time cook are paid staff members. Customers pay for the service which provides one hot meal and one cold meal a day. Citizens in two senior citizen housing projects are serviced.

Other examples could be given. As John B. Martin, former Commissioner on Aging, has stated, for people to be able to come together to eat in a group setting is a needed boost to both health and morale of older people.

The spiral of lowered income, lessened strength, and decreasing health continues at more rapid rate for the poor than for those with adequate incomes. Those people without sufficient funds to buy necessary foods soon exist on nutritionally inadequate foods. Studies in Rochester, New York, have shown that poor diets are more than twice as numerous for older families with incomes below $1,000 than for those with higher incomes.[3] Findings from other parts of the country substantiate these statements. For example, only one in twenty elderly persons among 695 in Linn County, Iowa, was found to have a nutritionally sound diet.

"Operation: Loaves and Fishes" was set up in some areas as a Community Action Program with the goal of providing nutritious meals and foods at low cost to the older people who live on marginal or poverty level incomes. In addition to providing the foods at either a central location or for taking home, the program aimed at stretching the limited incomes of the recipients by implementing surplus food programs, food stamp plans, and by educating the older people concerning marketing and other consumer education.

The employment of the older poor in the program was also a built-in component. Volunteer services were encouraged. Stemming from a project like this were many types of social action programs which dealt with money-saving matters in addition to those concerned with food. Once people were involved in the food program, their interest could be extended to other matters of consumer interest. Some topics which proved useful have been learning about mail order drug and pharmaceutical programs for the elderly, local discount programs in the area of furniture and clothes as well as foods, possible discounts for theaters and other amusement and recreation areas, reduced carfares and other transportation possibilities.

The persons who have spent most of their lives being poor and those who have grown poorer as they grow older can, through a program like Operation: Loaves and Fishes begin to overcome their sense of inadequacy and powerlessness and begin to take a hand in their own learning about nutrition and about other ways of bettering their life-styles.

ACTION

Some agencies having volunteer programs have been pulled together under the responsibility of President Nixon into a new governmental agency entitled ACTION. Encompassed in this effort, which is directly in the Office of the President, are Foster Grandparents, the RSVP (Retired Senior Volunteer Program), and SCORE (Service Corps of Retired Executives). Also the Peace Corps and VISTA, both of which enlist older persons, have been included in the ACTION program.

Foster Grandparent Program

At first glance they seemed a strange pair.

The old man was the color of chocolate, with hair like sugar powdering. His face showed the marks of pain and endurance of it.

The little boy had the fair skin of the institutionalized child and the big head of a hydrocephalic youngster. He was crippled and sat crookedly in his wheelchair. Only his clear green eyes darkly fringed looked alive.

The old man had once been a preacher, father of five, breadwinner. Now he was 84 and alone.

The boy had been fourth in a family of six and a burden. He had been in the State School for the Retarded more than four years. His family hardly visited him anymore. When he came to the School, he was without speech. Now he could say, "Dat's my granpaw," laying his too-large head against the dark hand. And the old man tenderly patted the white cheek.

One of a coterie of Foster Grandparents, the man had been recruited a year before. He and the boy had become friends from almost the beginning.

Now they were a pair. The boy waited in the morning for "Granpaw," and the old man was the first one out of the bus when they stopped at the State School. They might spend the morning "walking" together (with the old man pushing the boy in his wheelchair) to see the new-sprung daffodils or to smell a budding rose. They might listen for the call of a bird on the wing or sift through pebbles looking for treasure. They might sing, with the boy humming steadily, or they might just sit close enough to draw warmth from the sun and from each other. Sometimes the old man would help the boy dress or feed him his lunch. He taught him words and told him stories.

What did they mean to each other? They might tell it best. When asked who the old man was, the boy put out a hand. "He's mine—Granpaw."

The Grandfather was more articulate. "I've learned something I never knew before," he said. "First, I've learned a kind of patience I wish I'd had when my own children were little. And second, I've learned that there is love which can reach out much farther than the family."

The Foster Grandparent program, initiated by the Administration on Aging, has proved to be one of the most successful of the projects giving older people the opportunity to serve. Lower-income persons are recruited to work with children in institutions, including those for the retarded or disturbed, convalescent hospitals, or temporary care centers. The "Grandparents" are paid a minimum wage and are transported, generally, to the site of their work. They work approximately half time, but they bring a full-time and new quality to the lives of the children.

The "secret ingredient" infused by the Foster Grandparents is one of concern and individual attention. For children who have been confined to an institution and who have been but one of many, the appearance of a person who cares and demonstrates that concern is healing. Like water to arid ground, the Grandparents have brought young children to flower. Retarded youngsters who were not toilet-trained have learned to care for their own needs. Children who could not dress themselves have begun to put on their clothes. Some who were bedfast or who lay on the floor have patiently been helped to stand or to sit in chairs. Some now feed themselves; others have learned words. Every child has improved.

Perhaps what has happened to the Grandparents is even more dramatic.

One older man hesitated to try to work in the program. He

could not walk half the length of a football field without being totally exhausted. However, he started to work. At the end of the first six months, he reported that he could walk almost indefinitely with "his" child and never even feel winded. It is even rumored that they play ball from time to time, and "Granpa" outruns the boy.

A maintenance worker on one project reported that a Grandmother whom he knew had been moping around and feeling sorry for herself after the death of her husband. Then she got involved in the Foster Grandparent project. He says, "She started talkin' about her work and about the kids. She started sprucin' up some and she began to get back to bein' a human being. Now she even goes to the beauty parlor once in a while and I hear there's a fellow interested in marryin' her." [4]

Another report told this story. "I saw the cutest thing. Grandma S. was making ornaments while Myrna was beside her braiding nylon strips. Since she couldn't hold one end for Myrna as she was supposed to do, she had it pinned to her garter." [5] This technique was instituted by an 83-year-old.

Other stories abound. There was the retarded girl who was like a vegetable, and sat with eyes cast down all day long. A large girl with mop-strand hair, she was like a heavy rag doll. Where she was placed she remained. She might have been inanimate. Day after day her Grandmother brought her to the music room where other Grandmothers and "their" children played music and danced. She remained unmoving for weeks, but her Grandmother kept bringing her to the music room. One day she lifted her dark eyes a trifle. Another day she kept them up longer. It took a year before she rose from her chair one day when the "Here we go Loopy-Loo" song was started. She did not head for the group or acknowledge their presence. She simply stood and then sank back when the music had ended. Many weeks later she edged into the circle for that particular song. When the line "And turn yourself about" was sung, she awkwardly turned.

That was the beginning. From that point she began to speak and to take part in all of the activities involving music. She is no longer an inanimate object but a retarded girl trying to learn some simple skills.

The examples are many. In one project there is a pavilion which has been donated, and regular marches are held with speaker and amplifier mounted on wheels from a cast-off wheelchair. Elsewhere there are sewing rooms and workshops for building—and fun.

What happens in programs like the Foster Grandparent one is that "mutual miracles" frequently occur. For the children, the wonder may be in a profoundly retarded group where children who are mostly crib-bound begin to learn some head balance because a Grandparent has patiently worked with them in such development. Or the improvement may be spelled out in the fumbling fingers of a little boy who learns to use a spoon instead of fingers. At other times it may lie in a little girl's crippled fingers which are becoming stronger through the patient use of a tiny squeeze toy brought to her by her Grandmother.

The children's improvement demonstrates one miracle.

The other miracle comes as the Grandparents themselves change and improve as they work with the children. An 85-year-old Grandmother who suffered a broken hip and was thought to be "through" returned to work in four months, using a walker to aid her. An old man suffering from emphysema was not sure he would be able to perform any service. He and his "Grandson" now take short walks together, and the man has not had to return to the hospital since he started the job. They are only two of hundreds of Grandparents whose health has improved with their working.

The physical improvement in the Grandparents is a barometer to the mental health of the older people who, released from the prison of their loneliness and isolation, are able to bypass pain and discomfort and give of their love and talents and concerns to young people who need them.

There is an excitement about the days the Grandparents are due at their assignments. The children who can walk are pasted to the windows watching. And the Grandparents walk with fast step to reach the dormitories and the waiting children.

Retired Senior Volunteer Program (RSVP)

To be busy is important to older persons. But to be busy with meaning is restorative. Knowing that volunteer work has to have relevance and to call upon the special skills which volunteers might have to offer, the planners of the Retired Senior Volunteer Program took as their goal the development of significant volunteer service for older adults.

The program was set up under Title VI of the Older Americans Act. Grants to local communities help to support development of the program. While the volunteer work is nonpaid, small amounts can be given for out-of-pocket expenses such as transportation. The program is locally planned, operated, controlled, and supported.

Needs and interests of the senior volunteer take precedence over any other considerations in this program. Local organizations are encouraged to provide a wide scope of opportunities for the volunteers, and the older persons are enticed in many ways to contribute their time and efforts to help resolve local problems.

The volunteer in this program may have any type of educational and work background. However, efforts are made to match experience with assignment, and volunteers in this program have worked in schools, courts, libraries, museums, hospitals, nursing homes, day care centers, and institutions for shut-ins.[6]

A program like RSVP helps the older person to regain what Dr. Gordon F. Streib has called "role losses."[7] He explains that such loss occurs when the person's family has grown up and children have left, when income and health have declined. Into this void, and in order to continue to live a life with meaning, the person has to move ahead and to seek substitute kinds of roles which will give him some of the same kinds of satisfactions he received from his earlier positions.

As Dr. Streib has pointed out, the undertaking of such new roles requires flexibility and the exercise of initiative. As increasing attention is given to volunteerism as an activity for the over-60 generation, time is centered also on helping the older person to prepare emotionally for his nonpaid job.

One of the principles of the RSVP program is that the retired seniors could volunteer for any kind of job, so long as they did not replace someone in a paid position and so long as the efforts were not "made" work.

Service Corps of Retired Executives (SCORE)

The SCORE program draws together executives who are retired but who have skills they want to share with others. Such aid as these former administrators offer may be in simple bookkeeping or in the complicated structure of plant management. They volunteer on a time schedule selected by themselves and often are able to be the catalyst to help some low-income person make a successful venture into an independent business.

The SCORE program, like the others, has a dual benefit. For the inexperienced "beginner," the advice and suggestions of knowledgeable persons may give him both know-how and confidence. For the retiree, the challenge of working out possibilities in a business may keep him from stagnating or feeling useless. The Small Business Administration helps to implement the SCORE program, which is a nationwide program of free counsel and guidance by knowledgeable, experienced experts to small businesses already in existence and to persons planning new business ventures.

Composed of retired executives and former owners of businesses, SCORE includes lawyers, engineers, bankers, accountants, economists, plant managers, production analysts, and other specialists.

OTHER PROGRAMS

Funding sources are being reconsidered at this writing, and the following are programs which prior to 1973 had been funded by a variety of federal, state, and private sources.

SOS

The Senior Opportunities and Services program allows the elderly poor to help organize and manage their own projects. Originally funded through the Office of Economic Opportunity, the program helps to erase the stereotype that older people want to be cared for and do not like to be asked to plan for their own activities and future. Most of the numerous programs are administered directly by the community action agencies. In some instances non-OEO agencies such as Catholic Charities served as nondelegate agencies.

Proof that the stereotype of elders as dependent is false came with the Kirshner Report, which was a study of SOS made to OEO. Two of the findings reported were that the older the age of the person in the program, the more effective was the change that took place in him. Also, the older the age of the director of the program, the more significant was his own change.

The SOS program is nonspecific. Any project for which a senior citizen can qualify fits into the philosophy. Many of the efforts are in information and referral; others are direct action.

One of the most significant and comprehensive programs reported was organized as the West Central Missouri Development Corporation, which utilized 34 senior centers in a nine-county area. From their efforts have evolved four craft companies, centralized medical examinations, delivery of hot meals to the sick, and transportation to medical centers. Committees on social concerns keep track of legislation, and consumer education sessions are conducted. The latter activities are carried out through a Senior Senate, which serves as a problem-solving organization for thousands of old people who might otherwise be relatively powerless. Project FIND, described below originated within the sos program.

Project FIND

One program which was successful and has served as a model for others is Project FIND (an acronym for Friendless, Isolated, Needy, Disabled). Project FIND represented the major effort by the National Council on Aging to learn about the lives of the elderly poor, to find out what their greatest needs are, and to try to locate resources. Carried out by the National Council on Aging under a contract from the Office of Economic Opportunity, Project FIND was organized in twelve parts of the country. Local programs were instituted by community action agencies, and much of the work itself was carried out by almost 400 indigenous aides, who ranged in age from 50 to 85.

Although Project FIND was funded for only two years, 1968 and 1969, permanent organizations, services, and programs were started or stimulated by the project in every one of the twelve original communities. More than 100 facilities evolved from and remained in the communities.

The present interpretation of the project stresses nutrition and food stamp programs. The volunteer concept has been altered to include all kinds of volunteers instead of older people working for other aging persons. The Red Cross serves as the administrating agency, and the emotional tone of the program itself has altered considerably. The initial stage of the "new" FIND program has been concluded.

Let us see it as it was at the beginning.

The hurt child retreats, often so far that he cannot be reached by human contact. Sometimes he goes into the world of mental illness, into a fantasy land where all humans are walled away and sealed and only things and space and time are left. The mentally ill adult, too, moves into his inner world and removes himself from those who love, and loving, may give pain.

But the old person who is friendless and alone often makes a different kind of retreat. He loses the joy-producing persons one by one—a mate, then friends, close relatives. The objects go next—the home symbolic of years of living, the car, the savings account. Where does he go?

As the program got underway, it was soon discovered that the older people who were sought were indeed difficult to find. Many of them had disappeared, with their poverty in pocket, into rural areas or inner cities or places where they could not be located easily. The report states that

some were not so much lost as invisible, because nobody wanted to look. If too many of them frequented a cafeteria, where food was low in cost, and where it was possible to sit for a long time over a cup of coffee and a roll, younger people began to go elsewhere to eat, repelled by the sight of arthritic hands carefully counting out coins, dragging feet, and clothes unkempt or clumsily restyled. All too often even a friendly proprietor was obliged to change the rules or close his restaurant. Then the customers disappeared, to hot dog stands or to the hot plate in a furnished room.[8]

Project FIND, instituted to help show both need and grassroots concern, had the dual function of research and service. The communities chosen to participate in the study represented urban, rural, and mixed, and ranged from Watsonville, California, to New York City. In all, 43,878 persons responded. Of these 18,967 were older poor persons whose incomes placed them at or below the poverty line drawn by the Office of Economic Opportunity. The most disadvantaged among them were nonwhite women who were living alone, divorced, separated, or had never married.

Typical of the candidates for Project FIND was one old lady described thus by Betty Murphy:

Perched like a timid little bird afraid to fly, the 71-year-old lady stood on a curbstone in New York's lower West Side, peeking up at passers-by under a blue net bonnet while clutching a small purse with both hands. She was frightened because the landlord threatened to throw her out of the hotel room where she had lived for many years if she continued to bother him about making repairs. The faucets in the sink leaked so badly she had to go out and spend 39 cents for a sponge.[9]

The program itself was characterized by the two words "elderly" and "poor." As the National Council on Aging reported, some of the people sought were the poor who had grown old, while others were the old who had grown poor. Many of them, like the little lady described above, were "hidden" in little caves of poverty covered over by the growth of urban development. Others were abandoned in rural areas, where progress and private automobiles had left them stranded in shacks or rotting houses removed from neighbors or help.

The New York project workers stirred action among the elderly themselves. When several hotels on Times Square were about to be torn down, spelling eviction of 400 or more people over 60, the FIND staff spent weeks going into hotels day after day to find the older people facing eviction and to assure them that help would be given. Public meetings and a march to City Hall brought public attention. As the time for eviction neared, FIND staff members delivered affidavits of harassment to the Rent and Rehabilitation Commissioner's Office, and evictions were halted until a public hearing could be held. Finally, as a result, the Department of Relocation offered to help find new quarters for the tenants, and landlords were asked to guarantee a week's rent to help with the moving costs for those who did not have them otherwise.

The New York staff also assisted in passing legislation on behalf of older people, including rent stabilization laws and a rent exemption bill for certain eligible people. They opened a coffee house where older people could meet with a sense of dignity and companionship.

The multitudes of hidden old people who needed the services offered by New York's Project FIND were thus described by the director of the project:

So many are sick, crippled, and hungry. . . . And they are all invisible. They walk down the street with their whole life in two shopping bags and no one sees them.[10]

The outreach workers for the project proved that they are willing to search out the old and the poor pocketed away from sight. Many of the elders had never heard of Medicaid; most of them know nothing of food stamps. The FIND aides worked as volunteers far past their 20 paid hours per week. They made reassurance telephone calls, visited clients, provided transportation, and escorted persons to the doctors' offices or to do needed errands.

Senior AIDE *Program*

Informally designated as Senior AIDE (Alert, Industrious, Dedicated, Energetic) but known officially as the Senior Community Service Program, this project was beamed at helping to combat the low-employment, low-income status of many elderly poor. Conducted by the National Council of Senior Citizens, the American Association of Retired Persons (AARP), the National Retired Teachers Association (NRTA), and the National Council on Aging, with the help of the Farmers' Union, the program had two primary objectives. One was to provide socially useful part-time employment for low-income elderly persons. The second was to improve and expand existing community services—and to create new services. The project was expanded from a total of 40 persons in each of 10 community projects to 1,148 AIDES in 19 projects. Further expansion added nine additional communities, and the program was refunded in exact dollar amounts in 1970.

The Senior AIDES have been employed on jobs that are not generally available and would not have been open to the elderly. Applicants had to be 55 years of age or older and meet the Department of Commerce economic index guidelines. Mostly the Senior AIDES have been employed in person-to-person service. Basically, they have been expected to work in the following areas:

1. *To provide information regarding community services needed and available.*
2. *To provide assistance to elderly poor who are ill, shut-ins, or in need of physical help in getting around.*
3. *To provide services in schools, day care centers, libraries, senior citizen centers.*
4. *To assist in securing information for community research and development activities.*
5. *To assist in program planning for maximum training and utilization of the elderly in community organizations and Senior AIDE programs.*
6. *To assist public employment services offices in interviewing the elderly and in canvassing businesses in locating and developing part-time employment for the elderly.*
7. *To assist in supervisory, office, and similar services in public and private nonprofit organizations.*[11]

The Senior AIDES applicants were those who fit into two basic categories: the lifelong poor and the new poor. The lifelong poor were often members of minority groups and were frequently unskilled, underemployed, and poorly educated. The new poor were those who had been self-sufficient throughout their lifetimes but who were unable to care for themselves in their older years.[12]

The conclusions reached by the National Council of Senior Citizens concerning the Senior AIDES program was that those elderly persons who have comparatively good physical health and mental competence are able for and eager for employment in community service activities. Also, the community service organizations cannot provide all of the services they were intended to give because of limitations in the number of professionally trained staff and facilities. The AIDES serve to fill gaps. In addition, the outreach and person-to-person service which the elderly give in the AIDES program provide benefits to the persons providing the services, the persons served, and the community. The Senior AIDES also help the community agencies to carry on cultural, recreational, protective, and administrative services.[13]

Schools find the senior citizens invaluable in extending their program activities. In Winnetka, Illinois, members of a program entitled Project for Academic Motivation worked on a one-to-one basis with children needing help; they also lectured to entire classes or worked with small groups. In the public schools in Dade County, Florida, they help supplement the teachers' tasks in ways to help improve the various programs.

Public libraries were able to stay open longer in Vermont because senior library AIDES work there. In Michigan senior persons were tourist guides in the summer.

Private industry also has stepped into the picture. A private firm instituted job placement for older persons on temporary assignments. Others hired former employees to serve as guides through their plants. Senior Personnel Placement Bureaus were set up in Connecticut, while in Maryland an Employment Counseling Service made it possible for thousands of jobs to be filled by persons over 60.

In a special program sponsored by the Montgomery County Federation of Women's Clubs, a group known as Senior Home Craftsmen and Good Neighbor Family Aides worked in their own neighborhoods at part-time jobs. The senior craftsmen limited themselves to small home repairs, which would not be profitable to commercial contractors. The Good Neighbor Family Aides were generally older women who had been competent in homemaking in their own lives and who, with training from local Red Cross chapters, were able to render service to families needing help in the home where young children or older persons needed care on a temporary basis.

All of the above programs of service demonstrated that initiative and effort could produce the mutual benefits of serving a population which might otherwise be idle and isolated, while giving a kind of service which is needed badly by communities or individuals in them.

Built into most of these programs were the concerns of an organization which was willing to set up the working procedures for such efforts and which was then willing to offer special kinds of training to "shore up" the skills which the elder citizens possess. For each group, the programs fill a void.

Letters to the sponsors demonstrate the meaning of such efforts. For Mrs. Simpson the dual burden of a crippled retarded son and a seriously ill husband almost demolished her health. When her husband needed to be hospitalized, she was frantic. No ordinary "sitter" could cope with the boy, and her husband needed her at his side. It was at this moment that a trained Homemaker, Mrs. Farabee, 72, came to Mrs. Simpson and remained in the home to look after the son.

For Bobby Minter the program had a personal benefit. He didn't know how he got there, but old Mr. Miller started appearing in his classroom and helping him with his baffling reading problems. Bobby improved, and he and Mr. Miller became great friends. For Mrs. Randall it was wonderful to have someone who could fix her torn window screens and leaky faucets.

And they are only three of the thousands of people who have been able to live better because the mutual needs of people were met in a meaningful fashion.

Green Thumb and Green Light

In the Green Thumb and Green Light programs, originally funded by the Model Cities program of Housing and Urban

Development (HUD), low-income men and women work in rural areas to help beautify parks and roadsides. They also help in the schools and libraries and do outreach services.

In some Model Cities Areas they have manned day care centers. In one such neighborhood in Seattle the older men and women are employed to give direct service as home-makers and handymen to other residents.

In various states the Department of Labor working through the Farmers' Union has served as host agency. The work may be supervised by public or private agencies, depending on the structure of the project and the political policy of the state.

Serve and Enrich Retirement by Volunteer Experience (SERVE)

SERVE began as a research and demonstration project on Staten Island, New York, under the sponsorship of the Committee on Aging in the Department of Public Affairs of the Community Service Society. The venture was so successful that the State of New York continued to fund it after the Title IV grant from the Administration on Aging ended. By 1971 there were 38 pilot SERVE programs in operation in 19 counties throughout New York State.

Programs "for" groups of people often fail because of the implied and actual donor-recipient relationships. The expressed unhappiness of many retired people has stemmed from their feelings of uselessness. Programs planned by others "for" them have little appeal for those who are used to giving of themselves to others and who, by virtue of being retired, may have time to work on behalf of various populations.

The mutual benefits which accrued to those who volunteer and those who are aided were stressed continuously in the project. Both groups attested to the fact that the program works.

It all began in 1967 in the Community Service Society when questions were raised among the staff about whether or not persons sixty years of age and over could and would find satisfaction in volunteer service. Although there were some older volunteers at work, they generally had performed in those particular roles for years. Most of them, also, held moderate– to upper–middle-class standings. The pyramiding effect of such efforts can be shown in the fact that the Staten Island program was an extension of several other demonstrations which had been undertaken by the National Council of Jewish Women, Good Companion Volunteers of the Henry Street Settlement on the Lower East Side, and the findings of a Brandeis University study.

Built into the SERVE program was the idea of companionship at all levels. Recognizing the serious problem of isolation of the old, the planners made this program a group project. The older persons who were recruited serve in a group, although their assignments at the same agency might be individual ones. Such a plan permitted the expansion of companionship and discussions among the older volunteers themselves and allowed for easier modes of giving transportation to those who needed it. The in-service training was carried on by regular group discussions, thus stimulating thoughtful analysis and expanding the friendship role of the older persons themselves.

The imagination which it took to stimulate older persons to participate in such a program was evidenced from the beginning by the staff of the Community Service Society of New York. In assessing ways in which they might be able to find and recruit the older volunteers, they recognized that they would have to go to where the people were and would have to find some method of alerting and interesting those persons to participate in the program. As they examined possibilities of methods for bringing such people together, they looked for something which had already stimulated the concern of older people. With Medicare about to go into effect, they used that as a tool. Since the new benefits would be available to those who signed up immediately, the staff organized neighborhood meetings to tell older persons about the Medicare Program. At the sessions, members of the Social Security staff would answer questions, and members of the Community Service Society would explain about volunteer opportunities and the need that had been found for the services of older people.

Auxiliary and supportive methods were used. Personal explanations were sent to individuals; memoranda were mailed to community and religious leaders. Posters were placed in spots where they would be seen, and at the meetings the older persons were welcomed individually by a committee. In fact, every method known to personalize and stimulate the older person to volunteer for service was used.

During the three-year demonstration period, 642 men and women served actively as volunteers. Nearly half of the women and one-fourth of the men lived alone.

Other older volunteers worked for the program although outside its walls. They conducted mending sessions, prepared scrapbooks, and helped make occupational therapy materials. Many members of the group which performed these services were from a housing project composed mostly of low-income persons living in an isolated area.

What did SERVE mean to the volunteers and to the community? Participants attested to the fact that it brought the older persons into the activities of the community and gave agencies and institutions a new and meaningful look at the elderly. The volunteers have pointed out that SERVE has meant a new goal in life, or that it has led to community involvement, that they have developed from it a renewed sense of usefulness and a new outlook.

Syracuse Housing Program

Recognizing the need to eliminate the segregation of the old from the young, some housing authorities and private investors have built facilities which invite the mingling of the age groups. For example, in Syracuse, New York, the Syracuse Housing Authority maintains a 21-story apartment building for persons past 62 with limited incomes.

Immediately opposite the housing building is a similar one for Syracuse University students. In a lower building between the two high-rises are a modestly priced cafeteria and lecture rooms where various types of courses are held. Additionally a "match" program has been instigated. Sometimes the "match" takes the form of recreation which both enjoy, such as games of checkers or chess or musical duets. Sometimes the roles are complementary. The older person may be willing to do mending or other handwork for the young person who, in turn, will shop or run various kinds of errands for the older partner.[14]

In such a setting the artificial plans for bringing generations together are no longer needed. People are able to meet in natural ways and to indulge in human interaction without the self-consciousness of "representing" differing age groups.

Such a housing program can well be a model for others. However, the demand is far beyond the supply of this or similar developments. The Syracuse Housing Authority, for example, has a three-year waiting period for space available in the housing program, and building funds and means cannot keep pace with the requests for apartments.

When age groups are able to be together at junctures of interest, both populations benefit. The pattern, on a large scale, simulates an extended family setting and permits a kind of relationship which is often bypassed in the present culture with its nuclear families and placement of family members in geographical locations far from one another.

The protection offered by housing built for older people and the stimulation offered by contact with an age group alive and concerned with ideas might prove to be a model kind of setting which could be emulated on a large scale.

The "Friendly" Telephone

The telephone can prove to be more than a convenience for many of the elderly. For some it is a lifeline. Increasing technology, much of it spun off from the National Aeronautics and Space Administration, makes telephone conversations and dialing possible even for persons who are bedridden or immobilized.

Because the telephone can provide a kind of companionship to those who are removed from contact with others, many kinds of telephone programs have been begun. One of them in Davenport, Iowa, is "Dial-A-Listener." Here a person who simply wants to talk with others can dial a special number. Ten professional people, all of them elderly, are the listeners. This type of program, which has proved successful on college campuses and in suicide prevention, serves a special need when older people can talk to one another in this setting.

The benefits of service are utilized in Nassau County, New York, where persons living in nursing homes are themselves serving as the volunteers to call old people who live alone. The concept of service is revived for many of the nursing home residents who now know that they too can reach out to others, if only via telephone.

Many older persons live with the dread that they might become ill or fall and suffer injury without being able to contact anyone for help. A telephone reassurance program has proved useful. Here the person living alone is telephoned at a set time each day. If he does not answer, help is sent immediately to his home. Persons serving as telephoners may be from any age group or social setting. In some instances teenagers volunteer. In others, older people serve as callers. Businesswomen and clubwomen are the volunteers in some states, while churches provide the organizational structure for the program in others.

One woman who was rushed to the hospital because her

"caller" received no telephone answer is an advocate for the program. Since she has recovered, she has recruited a dozen other women to serve. For her, the telephone service was a lifesaver in a literal sense.

Friendly Visiting

In a culture which is urbanized, mechanized, and complicated many acts which were simple and expected in former times now have to be "organized" and planned. The Friendly Visitor program is one example.

The Friendly Visitor plan provides volunteers to see homebound and institutionalized persons on a regular basis, giving companionship and providing services such as writing letters or going shopping. Sometimes there are simply conversation and exchange of news; at others there may be a card game or checkers. The persons who engage in this program are always given an orientation in order that they can understand the needs of the home-bound person and respond appropriately.

Here again, older people have volunteered and have proved to be highly responsible and helpful to other elderly persons. All age groups have participated in the service, however. A schoolbus driver in Colorado delivers children to school, parks his bus, and makes "rounds" to several people who are living alone. In states as widely separated as Connecticut and California high school students have an "Adopt-a-Grandparent" program where they visit and run errands for their charges.

This program grew out of a service started in Chicago in 1946 when social workers, noting how lonely many of their clients were, tried to recruit volunteers to do some of the visiting they could not manage. Now the service is under the aegis of the Volunteer Bureau of the Welfare Council of Metropolitan Chicago.

For persons in rural areas and in out-of-the-way areas of the cities, the Friendly Visitor program infuses them with a new sense of participation and companionship. An interesting by-product of the service has been the improved health of the recipients of the service and their renewed interest in appearance and in management of their surroundings. Many old people who have silently waited for the final visitor now find that there is a life-giving friend who can be counted upon to provide companionship and help in numerous ways. With such a visitor anticipated, a person turns toward life again.

Transportation Efforts

Many innovative transportation programs are being instituted in efforts to bring more senior citizens to life-giving activity. One demonstration carried on from September 1966 through November 1969 was a mobile service conducted in Chicago, Illinois, and benefiting a total of 1,606 senior citizens. A total of more than 30,403 trips were made by the Senior Citizens Mobile Service and served to open lines of communications for withdrawn persons, to give feelings of independence, and to be a supportive service to other agencies.[15]

In Dallas, Texas, Senior Citizen Transit Cards are issued. For five dollars monthly, residents of Dallas County who are over 65 receive unrestricted riding privileges on Dallas Transit System buses during off-peak hours. A bill was signed into Texas law in 1971 permitting transit companies to provide reduced rate fares for old and disabled persons. Austin and San Antonio, Texas, boast good low-fare plans for older persons.

In San Francisco, the Bay Area Rapid Transit System extends into three counties and, because of the combined efforts of groups concerned with handicapping conditions in people and with the aged as a group, provides overall facilities for the elderly. For example, elevators move the nonambulatory or semiambulatory person vertically from street to train platform. Toilet facilities are designed to accommodate wheelchairs; stairs at the stations have handrails on both sides. A combination of loud-speaker directions and easily read signs aid the person with impaired sight or hearing.[16]

Reduction of transit fares and rerouting of transit were introduced in Santa Barbara, California. The plan was negotiated in 1969 between officials of the transit district and a coalition of senior citizens' groups. Medicare cards or special identification cards donated by the banks served as permits for reduced transit fares. The Community Action Commission of Santa Barbara County acted as sponsors.

In Tacoma, Washington, the City of Tacoma and the Council on Aging of Tacoma–Pierce County cooperated in a plan to permit senior citizens to purchase monthly passes for unlimited rides within the city. An understanding was reached that the project be carried on by voluntary effort without further cost to the city.

A minibus in Menlo Park, California, serves to bring older persons to and from Little House, a multipurpose center for senior citizens. Members are able to arrange for pickups by making standing reservations or by calling the day before. In addition to its runs to the center, the bus is used for special events trips. The bus itself is driven by Little House members who have undergone rigorous testing of their health and ability. About 500 riders a month take advantage of this facility.

The YMCA cooperated with the Administration on Aging in Chicago to set up the Senior Citizens Mobile Service. In this three-year demonstration, 48 agencies cooperated to help 1,606 elderly persons make a total of 30,403 trips. In this effort appointments were scheduled a day ahead, and a two-way radio permitted last minute changes. Some of the older persons reported that, because of this service, they had been able to leave their own neighborhood for the first time in years.

Government surplus vehicles have been mobilized in nine Missouri counties as a service to older persons. Originally funded by OEO, the program operates with paid staff and volunteers, many of them senior citizens.

Volunteers take their own cars to transport older persons in South Routt County, Colorado. Trips include getting the elderly to doctors' offices or to polling places. In Pennsylvania four rural counties combine services to give transportation via private automobiles.

Many cities have charged reduced rates for older persons. In some instances schoolbuses have been mobilized to run between school hours for the benefit of the older people.

These examples show some of the efforts which are being made to improve the ability of older persons to reach various facilities. It is imperative to recognize that the simplest tasks of living become obstacles to persons who do not have the mobility to go to the grocery store, the department store, or the doctor without exerting an extraordinary amount of effort and money. The simple joys of visiting with friends or attending sessions at various centers are often foresworn by aged persons who have no way of physically reaching out to others.

One suggestion included having Medicare cover the cost of local transportation for trips to doctors' offices, hospitals, grocery stores, and places of worship.[17] An alternative discussed was the possibility of having a separate federally financed program to cover the costs of essential transportation services. The term "Transicare" might be used.

The philosophy of providing adequate transportation for the elderly was stated thus by Louis J. Pignataro, ". . . all of these barriers must be overcome if we are to adequately serve the aged American. . . . The goal now is to permit the elderly to feel that they are leading normal, fruitful lives in a well-balanced community, not just existing in God's waiting room." [18]

To be able to transport the elderly from place to place is essential. To motivate them to leave their homes and move into the larger world is vital.

Legal Services for the Elderly

Mrs. Margolis, who has been living alone in the two-story clapboard house since Harry died, receives a notice that unless her back taxes are paid she will be subject to legal action. Terrified, hard-of-hearing, Mrs. Margolis does not know where to go for advice or help.

Miss Hildebrand has a different kind of problem. A book salesman found her one lonely afternoon and persuaded her to enroll in a book club. Miss Hildebrand signed the contract without reading it, and now she is being dunned and reminded that she owes the company $17.45 for back orders and a continuing amount of $8.00 per month. Miss Hildebrand doesn't have that kind of money, but she is frightened. What can she do?

For Mr. Foster the problem lies in his Social Security payments which were reduced about two months ago. He does not seem to be able to locate the right people to help him straighten out the matter.

Mrs. Johnson's landlord threatens to send her to the State hospital.

Mrs. Margolis, Miss Hildebrand, Mrs. Johnson, and Mr. Foster are only four of thousands of older people who are often victimized or problem-beset because of their age or financial condition. The Legal Research and Services for the elderly was originally funded by the Office of Economic Opportunity to try to give help to the older people in need of legal aid.

In South Miami Beach an exciting demonstration program was instituted. Funded as one of five projects in the nation and operated by the National Council of Senior Citizens, the South Miami work was designed to be a model for others. Legal paraprofessionals and lay advocates are used extensively. An advisory board serves as consultants. Overall they have helped to strengthen laws and regulations on nursing homes and to institute laws imposing safety rules in behalf of persons who live outside nursing homes but "in public lodgings of two or more stories that are inhabited by four or more persons incapable of self-preservation."

Adventures in Learning

Old people can't learn and don't want to try? That stereotype is erased daily by members of the Oliver Wendell Holmes Association. Drawing from the interest of older people who have backgrounds in business, the professions, and the arts, the Association has developed a program of "institutes." Leading the discussions are retired distinguished professors, and topics cover a broad range of ideas drawn from natural sciences and the humanities.

The plan emanated from New York, where the Paul A. McGee Fund supported the initial program. It has spread throughout the country, and local communities now organize and administer the institute under the sponsorship of and with the help of the parent association.

The institutes themselves may last only a few days or may extend for weeks. Participants are stimulated and encouraged when the institute is over to continue with their reading and discussion of the topics. No person is permitted to stagnate. While the Association leaders feel that the institutes are valuable in themselves, they also have the hopes that the older people from the institutes will be eager to become active and creative in the cultural life of their own communities.

The pilot institute which was set up at Rensselaerville, New York, was so successfully received that it now is on a permanent basis. Pilot programs have been tried in Arizona, Colorado, Florida, Kentucky, and other states. In Alaska an autonomous body has been generated successfully. Institute membership may range from forty to several hundred.

The stimulation of idea-exchange keeps participants alert and interested. The retired professor who has attempted to keep current in literature and art by reading every morning may find renewed insights and excitement from sharing some of the ideas in such an institute. The housewife who now has time and interest to learn about art can join with others in her age group to learn in exciting fashion.

"Nutrition of the mind" might be stated as the goal of this program.

Public libraries have joined in the efforts to offer "mind enrichment" for older people. In Dallas, Texas, books are taken to readers through the Extension Service Program. Almost 2,000 senior citizens living in retirement homes or active in various senior citizens' organizations are recipients. Volunteer "librarians" from the group are in charge of the collections, and new groups of books are brought and exchanged on a regular basis.

In Galveston, Texas, a library service is provided by the Rosenberg Memorial Library and provides tape recorded music and cassette players, along with film programs. A collection of oral history from senior citizens is also included.

Also in Texas, a program initially begun for the blind has been expanded to include persons with physical handicaps that interfere with reading. After a person has been qualified, he may use a free long distance service to obtain books and magazines in braille or extra large print, recordings on phonographs or cassettes, names of volunteers who record special material, reading aids, and special resource reading material on how to make the later years advantageous.

In practically every state public libraries are providing auxiliary aids for older people.

Information and referral services are often offered as part of health or welfare programs. Sometimes local organizations provide such information. In the state of Maryland, a toll-free telephone service has been instituted. Older people anywhere in the state can call in for information. The same procedure holds true for Westchester County in New York. In a six-county area of Kansas and Missouri an information and referral program was instituted.

The need identified was so great that the Administration on Aging undertook to develop a network of such programs as a major research and demonstration project under Title IV of the Older Americans Act.

A plan such as the informational one named can augment the other kinds of personal and telephone contacts. Mrs. Montgomery can bear witness to that fact. She and her husband had settled down in a small Texas city to enjoy Wilbur's retirement and their own advancing years.

When Wilbur died suddenly, she did not know where to turn. Without children or friends to advise her, she fumbled through papers and managed as well as she could. She had vague notions that some kinds of benefits might be due her, but she had no idea of how to get the specific information she needed. Fortunately, her pastor was aware both of her needs and of the services available. He advised her to make the necessary call where she learned that there were many services and benefits possible. She also was able to discover that there were groups who met together and socialized. In fact, the one telephone call opened windows to a new way of living.

Information and Referral

For many older people, knowing where to go for help or information can be a boost. In some communities services are available without the older person's knowing of them. Or, federal aid may be at hand if the old man or woman can request it. Too often the isolation of the elderly extends to every aspect of life. There are those who need medical help and have no knowledge of where such aid can be found. Others are eligible for Social Security but are unaware of how to go about getting the benefits.

And Still More

A "driver's refresher" course for senior citizens has been implemented in Texas by the Governor's Committee on Aging and the Department of Public Safety.

A Dallas bank, the Texas Bank and Trust Company, has offered a Preparation for Retirement Program, an eight-session course in evaluating and improving potentials for productive activity during retirement years.

Members of the American Association of Retired Persons and National Association of Retired Federal Employees in Texas took a four-day course taught by Internal Revenue Service employees and then volunteered to help elderly and retired persons fill out their income tax forms. The same group developed a consumer information desk to provide the general public, but mostly those in the older years, with knowledge in the consumer field.

Identification cards for senior citizens who no longer carry drivers' licenses have been developed in several states.

WHERE IS THE BEGINNING?

Imaginative and important programs have been begun and implemented in a variety of ways. Citizens concerned about their neighbors generally are the spearhead of most efforts. Sometimes the programs are encompassed under the sponsorship of an organization or institution. At others they fall within a governmental agency. Many of them have been started and carried out by local church members, by fraternal organizations, by labor groups, by senior citizens themselves, and by such groups as the American Association of Retired Persons, the National Retired Teacher Association, and the National Association of Retired Federal Employees. Local foundations have helped to implement some programs. City offices such as local parks and recreation departments have often been responsible for sponsoring senior citizen centers. Or, a local United Fund or other community coordination agency may serve as supporter for some ongoing program.

In other words, the will of the people—and the people at the local level—generally ignites the fire of action in development of community programs on behalf of older people. Many of the programs have begun as very small demonstrations involving a dozen people and have then expanded as they have shown their value and inspired others to emulate or help expand the work. Some of the food programs, for example, have developed from efforts made by a trio of church women who decided to provide meals on a trial basis for a dozen old people in the neighborhood. Other types of telephone reassurance, friendly visiting, transportation teams have evolved from needs discovered and then acted upon locally by persons who were concerned and involved in doing something for the old people needing help.

Where a state agency on aging exists, it may be a primary source. Working under Title III of the Older American Act, such an agency may have limited funds for demonstration programs.

The programs listed are only samples of what might be done. Each community has specific strengths and just as individual needs. Local people, alert to the needs, are the ones who can respond best and can help to use their own imagination and efforts in bringing forward programs of merit.

WHERE DO YOU LOCATE HELP?

If you are an older person wanting some specialized services or wishing to volunteer on your own, where can you turn? Or, if you want to begin a program, where might you go for ideas? Suppose you have the fundamental idea but need some funding, how can you find it?

The listing of state agencies on aging included at the back of this book provides a good beginning spot for anyone who wants answers to any of the three questions listed above. Particularly those individuals wanting ideas on what might be done or seeking resources for individual help might first contact the state agency on aging. Generally this agency has information on local resources and possibilities.

It is possible of course to contact directly some of the national groups mentioned, such as ACTION, the Department of Labor, or the various associations of retired persons. Churches, United Fund agencies, community councils, community mental health centers—any of these which exist at the local or regional level might be good informational sources for the person seeking facts about programs and aids.

CHAPTER SEVEN

Personal Responsibility

We are looking at the old in ourselves, in our neighborhood, in our country. What responsibility do we have for our own aging process, for that of those around us, and for society as a whole? This chapter will regard our total accountability for the elders in our culture.

"Stop the world; I want to get off" became the intriguing title of a play. In the speeding mechanism of today's society there are those who would at least slow it and alter it.

The machine of today's world has a "revved up" motor. "Faster" is the magic word, "saving time" the ideal. Speed reading has taken hold, and synopses are often touted as being better than the original.

Yet the culture which is going faster is also growing older. And old age can be the brakes on the speeding vehicle of the world.

Now is the time to look again at our old, especially those who are handicapped by poverty, color, or poor health. It is time to see them. And even as we look at "them," they are transformed and turn into ourselves. Like the beautiful woman in Shangri-La in the movie *Lost Horizon*, we become old and wrinkled and gray and ill when hit by the winds of time and age. In the inexorable march of the years we are the ones who slow the pace or halt the step, who turn into "them," who become the ones needing attention and service and understanding.

Thus, before we see our responsibility to others, we might take an inward look and find what we need to do personally to fill our own aging process with meaning and substance.

A LOOK AT OURSELVES

In his discussion of the life cycle, Erik Erikson talks of the *integrity* of the older person who has been able to live successfully through the seven stages of life and who now has "an emotional integration faithful to the image-bearers of the past and ready to take, and eventually to renounce, leadership in the present." Dr. Erikson points out that people who have made a good adaptation toward their own aging are able to have "a sense of comradeship with men and women of distant times and of different pursuits who have created orders and objects and sayings conveying human dignity and love." [1]

However, the person does not reach this stage of integrity and understanding without going through his own life cycle, facing each stage as it occurs, and maturing to the point that he is able to pass from one to the other. Thus, we can see that our own aging process depends largely and importantly on us at any age and on our ability to face that age realistically.

Dr. Erikson sums it up thus:

A meaningful old age, then, . . . serves the need for that integrated heritage which gives indispensable perspective to the life cycle. Strength here takes the form of that detached yet active concern with life bounded by death, which we call wisdom in its many connotations. . . . But the end of the cycle also evokes "ultimate concerns" for what chance man may have to transcend the limitations of his identity and his often tragic or bitterly tragicomic engagement in his one and only life cycle within the sequence of generations. [2]

In ancient mythology, as in earliest Biblical history, man or woman could emerge full-grown. Present psychology shows not only that man does not emerge as adult but that he must successfully have completed the "tasks of childhood" before he can be a mature and older human being. Often the aged person may be only a child in old man's skin, for the petulance or demands of old age may be simply vestiges of the selfish wishes of a young child, wishes that were not outgrown as the person grew older.

If we indeed in our culture want our older people to be as mature as possible and as self-sufficient, we have to start with prenatal training for parents and move along the spectrum of services through the life cycle. Most importantly, perhaps, we have to look at ourselves and at our rating on the continuum of growth and maturity.

If isolation is the ultimate abandonment, then involvement is the imperative commitment. As we have seen, old people who become removed from life often go into depression or other types of mental illness. Dr. Ira Iscoe calls it the "depletion of resources": part of the despair of old age. As older people are separated from family and close friends they may move farther from life into self-contemplation and hopelessness.

Where do we fit in? Each of us, right now, at our age and time? Right squarely into the middle of life, into involvement with other people, with projects with interesting pursuits. At any age and at all ages, we need to care—really care—about what happens to our neighbors, our cities, our civilization. And we need to act on that concern. The successful retirees we have looked at have been interested in and involved with persons other than themselves.

We do not acquire such concerns beginning at age 65. We cannot put aside "until we have time" our own development of interests in people and ideas. If we are going to spend our older years with a sense of commitment, we need to begin at this moment to practice basic mental health principles in the development of our own inner resources.

Total fulfillment is only a phantom. No one knows complete happiness for more than an instant at a time. Persons who are adjusted to life learn to cope with problems, to meet disappointment, to relish delights, and to work through their despairs. Everyone settles for less than his basic dream. Many try to shape reality in the image of the dream.

Various stages of life bring their own emotional difficulties. Adolescence is one such period. The middle years between 45 and 55 are another. Here, as we begin to see that we may never accomplish many of our goals, and as we realize that more of our life lies behind than ahead of us, we may go into temporary depression. Knowing that such depression is shared with others, we are able to be philosophical in our acceptance of the "gray" periods and of our endeavors to overcome them.

Growing old has little appeal for most of us. Yet it is the inevitable route of the "game" begun at birth. The problems posed and relationships examined in the preceding chapters are not, as we have seen, unique or disparate. They are instead only one shading of the rainbow of which life is comprised. Goethe said, "When I finish, I begin." Those of us who age successfully follow that basic idea. No one event, short of death, should be an ending. Retirement, marriage of children, crises—all of these can be stimuli to growth, which is a continuing process going on throughout the life cycle.

A LOOK AT OUR NEIGHBORS

Having seen that we have a responsibility for our own graceful aging, let us now look at our obligation to those around us —family, neighbors, or friends. All of our lives are intertwined; and if old age is to be pleasant for us, it must, of necessity, be good for those with whom we come in contact.

What then can we do in our neighborhoods and communities to see that others are cared for and helped to meaningful participation in life?

For one, we can aid them in partaking of activities. That a sense of being a participant in life is needed by all people is a fact emphasized in a report by the American Medical Association. Stress itself may be vital to the maintenance of health. In the Association report it is stated that "we are constantly bombarded with the case histories of corporation executives who 'keel over' from the 'tension' and 'pressure' they are subjected to. But we don't hear about those individuals who waste away quietly from the lack of tension or stimulation of any kind." [3]

Further, the report states,

A sense of purpose and the opportunity to contribute to others—these are as vital to total health as are adequate nutrition and rest. Whether this opportunity is thwarted by family members who deny the older members a voice in the family council, who are over-protective and relegate him to the role of "puttering," whether thwarted by the community which refuses to utilize the capabilities and contributions seniors can make to all aspects of community life; or whether thwarted by employers who refuse to hire after a certain age or retire persons at arbitrary chronological age . . . the results are equally detrimental to physical and mental health.

The need of centering older people in the heart of life has been stated thus by Will Durant, "To be busy is the secret of grace, and half the secret of content. Let us ask not for possessions, but for things to do."

Therefore, as a first step, we help to involve older people around us in life pursuits. We see to it that they are included in activities and are enticed into volunteering for projects. This we do for individuals whom we know.

But we reach farther than our immediate acquaintanceship. We examine our community, really study it to see what kinds of health facilities and nursing homes exist for older people. We learn about our poverty neighborhoods and find out what resources are present for old people. We look at transportation, food stamp programs, recreation, old age assistance, and welfare in order to know if there are silent "pockets" of isolated older people around us. Also, we volunteer our own services on behalf of such people in order that we can make our communities good for people of all ages. We look at our town also to see its activities for the young as well as for the old. We know about schools and other educational projects. We find out about recreation endeavors for persons of all ages.

We concern ourselves with others of every age, but we give special regard to the silent ones who cannot speak for themselves.

A LOOK AT OUR SOCIETY

Finally, then, we look at our society to see its actions toward all of the needy, including the aged, and to learn how we can help to shape and change its attitudes toward those people.

The problem of growing old itself is not new. People have always aged, in every culture. The problem lies not so much in the process of aging as it does in society's attitude toward those who have grown old. Legislation and appropriations are not enough. Revised attitudes and actions are needed to effect positive changes.

As our country ages, and as we age with it, we find that we must face, quickly, the multiple kinds of problems which come with early retirement, a growing older population, the deprived elderly, and need for leisure-time activities. The difficulties which have been set out as applying to "them" apply equally to "us." The 42 million middle-aged Americans, more than 18 million men and women aged 55 to 64, are at the heels of the "older citizen" category. Right behind them are the nearly 24 million men and women aged 45 to 54 who are already finding out that their age is a barrier in the job market and who are caught in the squeeze between longer years and shorter times of working.

It has been said that there is now a new kind of generation gap, for those 65 and over and those below it. At times the gap seems to be at least as serious as the one between young people and those who are of the preceding generations. Yet gaps can be filled; even rivers can be bridged if persons on each side are eager to reach out to those on the other shore. It is even possible to recognize that persons who are older can themselves dream dreams and can share those dreams with others.

In order to help make life better for people of all ages we need to recognize those factors in our society which exert a negative influence on the mental health of older people. The first of these, according to Dr. Stanley F. Yolles, is the generally unfavorable attitudes which are held toward aging and the elderly. The identity crisis suffered by many old people is characterized as occurring because they have lost the characteristics which are most important to their sense of personal identity and integrity. Doubting those qualities, older people then may simply give up and resign themselves to the status which society seems to place on them.[4]

The second point made by Dr. Yolles was that we need to understand and accept the dynamic, continuing nature of the aging process. Too many of us do not.

A third aspect is the need to accept older individuals as constituting an extremely heterogeneous group. Dr. Yolles points out, in addition, that in order to maintain the sense of values and integrity on the part of the aging we must preserve their right and opportunity to make the decisions which have bearing on their own welfare and activities.

"The concept of prevention must not be limited to programs outside institutions," says Dr. Yolles. "If prevention means the maintenance of the optimum functioning ability of the individual, then it has serious implications for programs within institutions."[5]

The establishment of the Community Mental Health Center program of the National Institute of Mental Health has been pointed out as one of the most important possibilities for bringing significant care for the elderly into every community. The Centers, philosophically, are supposed to provide essential mental health services to all age groups within the catchment area covered by the Center.

There can be no healthy community unless all age groups are nourished. Where there is discrimination, poverty, and racism, mental health withers. For good mental health is a flower which must be planted in the soil of overall community well-being and nourished with the sunlight and water of concern and striving on behalf of all the people.

Society can and must take responsibility and definite action, and Dr. Gerald Caplan has shown some specific ways in which the community housing the older people can respond to their needs. In the context of primary prevention of mental disorders such action is imperative.

Although he talks of three kinds of basic supplies needed—physical, psychosocial, and sociocultural—the last-named encompasses most of the societal responsibilities.

What do they entail? Let Dr. Caplan speak:

Social action in this regard again focuses on altering legislation, regulations, policies, and community attitudes and practices so as to promote a community-wide influence. A significant opportunity for preventive action lies in modifying retirement laws and regulations so that older people who retain their capacities are not forced to retire prematurely and so that in certain government departments and industries there may be part-time or lighter work opportunities. This would allow old people to continue working within the limits of their diminishing capacities for as long as possible. At the same time, old age assistance and retirement pensions should take up the slack in income, but should not be regulated in such a way that a person is penalized for earning extra money.[6]

In the prevention of social isolation, Dr. Caplan adds:

a preventive program should emphasize communal social and recreational facilities, which should be administered so that independence and the activity of the old people will be stimulated, rather than encouraging them to become the passive recipients of care . . .[7]

Dr. Caplan urged also that legislators and administrators be encouraged to help provide resources for populations "at risk." Upgrading methods of maintaining older people in their homes, neighborhoods, or communities can help to lessen the deterioration which comes when they are removed to institutions and become anonymous patients.

One more imperative function must be filled by each of us if we are to help society change its attitude toward the aged and assist the old themselves in finding meaningful patterns of living. This final charge is to be vigilant in observing the programs which are instituted on behalf of older people and to help them continue operation. Too often experimental projects are started, their value is demonstrated, and then they are dropped for lack of funding or support. Within these pages many worthwhile programs have been described; their value has been tested. It is incumbent upon all of us who are truly concerned with the betterment of conditions for all people to see that such projects are not lost by default or indifference.

It has been said that if one wants to know how a civilization behaves, he need only look at the way they treat their aged and their young. Each of us will be measured against that yardstick. We often adjust our steps to match the smaller ones of the child, but we seem less willing to do that for the old.

Yet we are looking not at different people when we see the infant and the octogenarian. In the baby we can see the coming of age and the inevitable shaping of skin and eyes and hair which age molds upon each person. In the old we can also view what was the child. We can see the shades of new wonder in the eyes and hear the echoes of fresh delight in the timbre of the voice.

They are one. It has been said that the world changes even as we stand on it. So do its people. And the small child and the old person stand together. Together they melt into a single human being, a being for whom we show concern.

Civilizations can be measured by the meaning they give to the full cycle of life because this kind of meaning pervades the thinking of the next generation, says Dr. Erikson. He states:

To whatever abyss ultimate concerns may lead individual men, man as a psychosocial creature will face, toward the end of his life, a new edition of an identity crisis which we may state in the words, "I am what survives of me." From the stages of life, then, such dispositions as faith, will power, purposefulness, competence, fidelity, love, care, wisdom . . . also flow into the life of institutions. Without them, institutions wilt; but without the spirit of institutions pervading the patterns of care and love, instruction and training, no strength could emerge from the sequence of generations.[8]

Parts of every person's life live on in the hearts of others, in the memories which other people carry of good deeds or certain activities. As in cremation, the nonessentials of life are burned away, and all that is left is the ash of goodness and of kindness and of gentle reaching out which then is scattered over many people. Just as the hurt child grows to hurt his own children, so the loved child or adult is able to give love to others and thus to start a cycle of worthwhileness in other persons' hearts.

Finally, then, we see the old in our culture. In them we see ourselves; we view the past and project into the future. We know that life is encircled by a single band composed of all ages and people of all languages and all colors. We are the young and the old, the donors and the receivers.

The heart of life beats within us only so strongly as it can beat for all the other people around us, the old as well as the young. The newborn infant is already old with seeds of yesterday and the generations before him. The octogenarian is young, young with the seeds of goodness scattered in the winds of time and taken root in other persons and other places.

Kahlil Gibran has summed this philosophy thus:

Yet the timeless in you is aware of life's timelessness,
And knows that yesterday is but today's memory and tomorrow is today's dream . . .
. . . yet who does not feel that very love, though boundless, encompassed within the center of his being, and moving not from love thought to love thought, nor from love deeds to other love deeds?
And is not time even as love is, undivided and paceless?
But if in your thought you must measure time into seasons, let each season encircle all the other seasons,
And let today embrace the past with remembrance and the future with longing.[9]

Against the impetuous and demanding cries of the very young, the voices of the old are faint. Yet it is the ears of the listeners which need to be attuned to hear the quiet falling of the tears or the lonely sobs of the helpless or the faint groans of those in pain.

We have spoken of the old. We have spoken of ourselves. We "ask not for whom the bell tolls," for we know that the bell of aging tolls for us all and that it is up to us to help bring about the changes which are needed for older people in our culture today and then for those of tomorrow.

What happens to the old in our culture—what happens to us—is of our doing in this time and this place. We hold the tools to fuse yesterday and tomorrow into a single torch.

A Young Person Responds

I see you, old woman. I see the *You*, not the old. In your eyes I read the story of the years, of the pain, the sweet delights, the tender pain. I see you, *Woman*, know your femininity, your graceful movements, your healing tenderness.

I uncover the swathing of the age and view you young and human and womanly. If I see you, if I can feel your pain, if I can know your joy, you are not alone. You are not a small "i" far away like a stringless kite.

I know you, woman. Your blood flows in me. I am of your soul. The dreams you dreamed have come alive in me and in those around me. Your wrinkled flesh grows firm on me. Your dried seed takes life. For if we are not part of one another, if we cannot carry forth delights and dreams, we do not live collective lives but die apart in singular death.

Look at me, woman, as I look at you. See—we know each other; we are part of the same rainbow. Your colors flow into mine; mine fade into yours. We are the same combination of sun and rain and reflection of life.

There are those who look at you and say, "She is childish." But I view you, look into the depths of your eyes, and I say, "She is child-like." To be childish is to be petulant, temperamental, unwilling to endure frustration or punishment or misery of any kind. But the slashes which make parentheses around your mouth show pain long endured and seldom vocalized. Your eyes bear imprints of tears shed and sorrow felt. Those are not the symbols of childishness. Yet you are childlike. For along with the signs of hurt and tolerance I view also the quick lights reflecting delight at life's newness. There are traces of laughter, and in your age and your tiring body there still resides the child who can awake to wonder and to the miracle of a light which is just beginning to trace gold lines on the wall of a room.

You are child-like, old woman, in your marvel at today's dawn.

Old woman, I do see the you that was and the you that is. I see you young and vigorous, full of family and love and the busyness of baking and soothing and training and cleaning.

I see you in the nursery rhyme. You still remember it, "There was an old woman who lived in a shoe . . ."

It wasn't exactly a shoe you lived in, but it seemed crowded like one when the children were young and the walls rocketed with noise and the beat of swift-swing music. When the stairs were lined with skates and books and spring-green sweaters. When the kitchen was jammed with youngsters opening the icebox, inspecting the cookie jar, leaning on the drainboard to watch the supper process.

"There was an old woman . . ." You weren't old then. You just felt it at times when fatigue nibbled at the calves of your legs and beat against your spine. You were only old against their youth, their exuberant, endless, energy-filled youth.

But now you are an old woman. And the shoe is empty. Walls quiet as watchmen on the corner. Stairs waxed, shining, empty. Kitchen big and peopleless. No smell in the kitchen except soap and disinfectant. No sound in the house. Just an old woman and an empty shoe.

You still have so many children you don't know what to do. Mainly because each child has the solution to your old age.

And no solution fits you, any more than someone else's shoe can match your foot. Each child wants to uproot you, place you in a new shoe, in one which has not softened to your shape with the passing years. No one could know that, quiet as the old house is, it still holds within its walls the long-forgotten sounds of a young boy's laughter or a tiny girl's sobs.

This is the shoe which you feel will fit you until you die. You want to stay where memories are echoes which sound at night. You want to gather all the years into the pocket of your self and hold them to you gently, fondling them like beads in the rosary of your life.

You will not wither in total loneliness—solitary, away. My hands and those of people around me will reach for you in the dungeon of your alienation, will lift you, carefully, into the slanted sunlight of our lives.

Our fires will bring you warmth; our companionship will give you sustenance. We will widen our circles. We will sprinkle you with our laughter; we will feed you with our concern.

Our children will touch you; the flushed warmth of their hands will penetrate your own.

We will open doors and invite you into the room-brightness of our lives.

I see you, old woman. But even as I look, your face turns into my own. We stand at opposite ends of the same long corridor, reflecting the image of one another.

I embrace you, old woman. And as I do, I honor my infants and those to come, my neighbors wherever they are, and the dawn which hides behind the nighttime of the present.

The 1971 White House Conference—and Beyond

White House Conferences, which have been held since early in the century on behalf of children and older people, can be either a guide to action or an exercise in polemics. Pledges are given; promises made. Sometimes a mutual sharing of ideas becomes a lever to positive movement. What happens as a result of the 1971 White House Conference will be written over the years by the people who urge follow-through programs in their communities and with their legislators.

Many of the programs mentioned in this book are pilot projects. Others may become permanent. Some have been vetoed; some remain unfunded.

Behind the 1971 White House Conference lay the broad purposes of creating a greater awareness of the older population, developing a comprehensive national policy on aging and support for it, and strengthening the means of older people for independent living and active participation in the life of the nation. It was hoped that a comprehensive body of national policies would evolve from the conference and thus give direction to action on behalf of older people at the national, state, and community levels.

Progress on behalf of the elderly *has* taken place, but it is only a beginning. Dr. Wilma Donahue, who was Technical Director of the 1971 White House Conference on Aging, gave a historical perspective of the 1961 White House Conference and a charge for the future concerning the mental health needs of older people.[1] She went on to say that the call for "certain positive concepts" was filled only in limited fashion. Pointing out that the Mental Health Centers program which was begun, Medicare and Medicaid, and the Older Americans Act all served to be of some significant help to older people, she added that not all of them had worked yet for the total interests of old people or for their mental health care, nor had the Older Americans Act led yet to a coherent national policy.

In delineating the mental health needs of the elderly, Dr. Donahue says:

We know much more about mental illness of elderly persons now than we did when the 1961 White House Conference recommended specific actions. We know that physical illness is very often the basis of mental illnesses and that treatment must begin with correction of the physical disability. We know that to evict the elderly mental hospital patient and re-house him in a nursing home or similar institution where only minimal physicians' services and no psychiatric services are available is not good social or medical practice.[2]

The White House Conference on Aging was set up to look at many of the needs of the older population and, at the same time, to see some of the ways in which citizen efforts could be directed toward changing, revising, or upgrading many of the conditions which exist for the population above 65. Meeting and documenting needs is important, but only as an initial step. The continuation of programs at every level of life, from the individual to the federal, is vital to the success of work on behalf of the population in need.

Similar White House Conferences have been held in the past. The real answer to questions raised, however, comes not at the meetings but with the action taken after the sessions have ceased. Just as it is not others about whom we are talking but ourselves, so it is not "they" who will institute the programs for older people, but "we" who have to make sure that they happen. The responsibility lies not beyond us but indeed within us.

HISTORY

The 1971 Conference marked the second conference so designated, the first being in 1961. Before that, in 1950, a "National" Conference on Aging was held in Washington, D.C. At the time of the initial conference, approximately 11.5 million people over 65 lived in the United States; by the 1961 Conference, there were about 16 million. The 1971 session saw 20 million older persons represented, or one in every ten Americans.

In the 1950 meeting called by President Harry S Truman, 816 persons came from all parts of the country. They talked about 11 broad subjects and developed recommendations which were to serve as guides to action over the next ten years. President Truman had charged the group with helping to find solutions to the problems of the aged.

The second White House Conference was preceded by a bill by the late Congressman John F. Fogarty calling for such a meeting. By September it had passed both Houses of Congress and was signed by President Dwight D. Eisenhower. During the two years of 1959 and 1960 much planning was done. At least 35 states held State Conferences on Aging, and about 73,000 people took part in some 256 regional meetings and about 760 county and community sessions. By the time all of the participants were totaled, it was estimated that some 100,000 to 200,000 people were involved in one way or another. More than 3,000 delegates attended the conference. Medicare was the most heated topic of the conference, although many controversial items were discussed in the subgroups.

In less than seven years efforts were started for another White House Conference. Senator Harrison Williams, Jr., of New Jersey, with the cosponsorship of some 15 other senators introduced the resolution asking for a second such conference. Both Houses approved a Joint Resolution, and President Lyndon B. Johnson signed it, making Public Law 90-256 an instrument for the convening of the session. The wording of the Joint Resolution is as follows:

Whereas the primary responsibility for meeting the challenge and problems of aging is that of the States and communities, all levels of government are involved and must necessarily share responsibility; and it is therefore the policy of the Congress that the Federal Government shall work jointly with the States and their citizens to develop recommendations and plans for action, consistent with the objectives of this joint resolution, which will serve the purposes of:

1. Assuring middle-aged and older persons equal opportunity with others to engage in gainful employment which they are capable of performing; and

2. Enabling retired persons to enjoy incomes sufficient for health and for participation in family and community life as self-respecting citizens; and

3. Providing housing suited to the needs of older persons and at prices they can afford to pay; and

4. Assisting middle-aged and older persons to make preparations, develop skills and interests, and find social contacts which will make the gift of added years of life a period of reward and satisfaction; and

5. Stepping up research designed to relieve old age of its burdens of sickness, mental breakdown, and social ostracism; and

6. Evaluating progress made since the last White House Conference on Aging, and examining the changes which the

*next decade will bring in the character of the problems con-
fronting older persons . . .*[3]

As planning began on the 1971 White House Conference,
it was decided, first of all, that older persons should have increasing roles in setting out their own plans and destinies.
Also, there was recognition that the poor older people must
have a voice. The changing development was expressed thus
by John Martin, then Federal Commissioner on Aging,

*The White House Conference on Aging in 1971 will differ
from the 1950 and 1961 conferences in the degree to which
older people are given the opportunity to express their desires and needs. For the first time in a national conference,
older people will be given priority and be involved in a major
way.*[4]

Beginning at the local level, forums were held at which
ideas and needs were discussed. Next were community forums for open discussion of needs and gaps concerning services for older Americans. Town meetings brought together
varieties of people in thousands of communities. These community forums were followed by state conferences, where the
local ideas were distilled into working papers for the national
conference. The White House Conference, called by President Richard M. Nixon, was charged with making specific
recommendations not only to the federal government, but
also to government at other levels and to the private and voluntary sectors as well.

This "three-year conference" was planned to be rounded
out with a followup year in 1972 during which the drive for
greater public awareness in and concern for the needs of
older Americans would be intensified. Action at all levels was
to be sought, and the planners hoped that new thrusts would
be made to give aid and service to those older people who
had been receiving it.

Thirty-four hundred delegates attended the White House Conference; they were truly representative of hundreds of thousands of persons who had participated at the local and state sessions and had been charged with the task of "speaking to the nation."

Fourteen major divisions were organized, with subsections under each one. Topics discussed were the following: Education; Employment and Retirement; Physical and Mental Health; Housing; Income; Nutrition; Retirement Roles and Activities; Spiritual Well-Being; Transportation; Facilities, Programs, and Services; Government and Non-Government Organization; Planning; Research and Demonstration; and Training.

Special Concerns Sessions also convened during the days of the Conference and wrestled with the following topics: Aging and Blindness; Aging and Aged Blacks; Asian American Elderly; The Elderly Consumer; Mental Health Care Strategies and Aging; The Older Family; Homemaker–Home Health Aide Services; The Elderly Indian; Legal Aid and the Urban Aged; Long-Term Care for Older People; The Poor Elderly; Rural Older People; Spanish-Speaking Elderly; The Religious Community and the Aged; Physical and Vocational Rehabilitation; Volunteer Roles for Older People; Youth and Age.

More than three thousand strong they came to the White House Conference. There were those who represented the people for whom the Conference was designated—the old, poor, and dark-skinned. There were those who would not be part of the older group for more than four decades. Some people were in wheelchairs; others shuffled on arthritic legs or used crutches or walkers. The youth bounded along the hotel corridors, hurrying to meetings, catching the escalators up or down—or rushing up the stairwells when they were crowded.

Women in dresses made by hand carried shopping bags of papers and materials, along with knitting. Sophisticates with attaché cases and designer suits walked beside them. The

dining rooms in the hotels were filled with delegates, and
people of varying age groups, socioeconomic levels, and
different parts of the country seated themselves side by side
and began comparing notes about the Conference and what
they hoped would be accomplished in it.

Six hotels were filled with delegates, and the constant shuttle buses were seldom empty as people went from home base
to special session to luncheon meeting. An Open Forum the
second night of the Conference permitted several hundred
people to stand before their peers and to express particular
concerns and hopes regarding the Conference and the activities on behalf of older people.

Senators and congressmen were main speakers at the
luncheon sessions, and general sessions featured well-known
keynote addresses. The activity was constant.

There were those who had given years of study to the
aging and the poor. Persons with advanced college or medical
degrees talked of gerontology and current research and
findings. There were those who had not been to school at all
but had grown up in shacks in the Piney Woods or bayous.
They spoke simply and from their own experience. Then
there were the students and young workers, fired by the
needs they saw, eager to take action, to move on behalf of
older people.

Some persons spoke with assurance. Others listened and
raised their hands timidly when it was time to vote.

But all were involved and all concerned.

Each recommendation presented was to be tested against
these criteria:

Is it based on knowledge and the recognized needs of older
people?

Is it consistent with established national goals and the values of society?

Is it feasible in terms of current knowledge, technology,
and manpower?

Is it clear?

Is it realistic in terms of present and future costs?

Will the general public and the decisionmakers support it?

Will it benefit other elements of the population?

Will it preserve the dignity, freedom, and right of choice of the older people?

Does it fix responsibility for action on a specific institution or agency?

Deliberations were earnest in the small groups of thirty or so people, and everyone had the opportunity to air opinions and to speak of needs and hopes and gaps in service. At least twelve hours of the Conference schedule were devoted to 95 separate and simultaneous discussions of the needs and problems of the Nation's older population.

PRE-PLANNING

The year before the 1971 White House Conference specialists on aging began to write background papers outlining the present situation for older people in the various areas designated. Papers were prepared also on examination of services, facilities, and programs; planning and evaluation; training; research and demonstration; government and nongovernment organizations.

Fourteen technical committees made up of knowledgeable professionals began in the fall of 1970 to study the background papers and to delineate the topics to be discussed at the Conference itself.

Nearly 400 national organizations made plans to participate in the White House Conference. Many of them were represented on various task forces assigned to making recommendations. Some of the groups, like the National Retired Teachers Association, issued their own policy statements based on the topics marked for Conference discussion. The Executive Director, Bernard E. Nash, speaking of the National Retired Teachers Association and the American Association of Retired Persons stated,

Our Associations with memberships of over 3,200,000 persons are keenly aware of the problems and needs of the elderly and are actively engaged in effecting changes to enhance the well-being of all older Americans. . . . We hope that the 1971 White House Conference on Aging will convene in an atmosphere of urgency and that the Delegates will realize the need for forceful action. We believe that this Nation has the will, the energy, the talent—not the least of which are older Americans themselves. The time has come for us to use them. That is the purpose of the Conference.[5]

A national policy on aging was a primary need declared by the group of retired persons, who felt that it was not possible to rely on diverse governmental programs without a high priority and focus to carry on the important work of directing programs for the aging. The Delegates were charged to help see that the postconference year was a year of action in which the recommendations were acted upon by the government and the private sector.

Working on the premise that there needed to be a philosophical backdrop for deliberations, the Associations of Retired Persons drafted a Declaration of Aging Rights, which they included in their booklet of policy statements. It reads thus:

Humanity's fundamental rights are life, liberty and the pursuit of happiness. They are rights that belong to all, without regard for race or creed or sex. We declare that all people also inalienably possess these rights without regard for age.

As love and nourishment are due the infant, as education and guidance are due the child, as freedom to work and build and lead are due the grown man and woman, so also are certain conditions of justice due our older or retired citizens. Among these, we declare to be:

1. The right to live with sufficient means for decency and self-respect.

2. The right to move about freely, reasonably and conveniently.

3. The right to pursue a career or interest without penalty founded on age.

4. The right to be heard on all matters of general public interest.

5. The right to maintain health and well-being through preventive care and education.

6. The right to receive assistance in times of illness or need or other emergency.

7. The right to peace and privacy as well as participation.

8. The right to protection and safety amid the hazards of daily life.

9. The right to act together to seek redress of their grievances.

10. The right to live life fully and with honor—not for their age, but for their humanity.[6]

It was against such a background philosophically that most delegates assembled to try to wrestle with the mammoth needs and concerns. They were charged not only with listing what needed to be done but with stating ways in which real and meaningful action could eventuate from the proposals.

SOME RECOMMENDATIONS

One recommendation which threaded the 14 sections, 95 subsections, and several special concerns sessions was that there be established some central agency within government to take responsibility for the aging and their needs. The majority of the groups felt that there needed to be a central office on aging in the Office of the Chief Executive, with responsibility for coordinating all programs and activities dealing with the aging, fostering coordination between governmental and nongovernmental programs directly and indirectly engaged in the provision of services, and for planning, monitoring, and evaluating services and programs.

Also, at the federal level, the central office should be implemented with the authority and funding levels and the full-time staff needed to formulate and administer policy. The group recommended that an advisory council should be part of the complex.[7]

One specific recommendation which grew out of the Task Force on Government and Non-Government Organization stated that the relationships between agencies in aging and other public agencies should be characterized by mutual adjustments and cooperation at all government levels and by durable joint agreements of responsibility for research, comprehensive planning, and provision of services and facilities, and should be based on and directly responsive to older Americans' opinions and desires at the grass root levels.[8]

In the great complexity of modern society, the Task Forces recognized that any efforts would have to combine governmental and nongovernmental resources, as well as large organizational plans, together with individual efforts in order to organize and implement plans which would be meaningful on behalf of older citizens. Coordination of agency efforts was also recognized as a necessary component of putting together comprehensive programs.

This particular Task Force summed up its recommendations as follows:

The preceding policy proposals of the Section on Government and Non-Government Organization clearly indicate the need and mandatory responsibility for every level of government, as well as of the private and voluntary sectors, to see to it that the organizational structures are revised to make possible effective implementation of the proposals and concerns of all of the other Sections of the Conference. The policy proposals repeatedly stress the need for ongoing advocacy at all levels of government and within the private and voluntary sectors. Also, relatedness and communication are recognized as essential ingredients of implementing plans for the elderly.

*Finally, these proposals place strong emphasis upon a focal
point at the top levels, within Federal, State, and Local Gov-
ernments, which will ensure the most effective support by
both the executive and the legislative branches of govern-
ments, and thereby of all private and voluntary agencies and
organizations.*[9]

What is the scope of the health problem for older people in
this country? The Special Committee on Aging in the United
States Senate put it this way:

*Health care costs keep going up for all Americans. But for the
older person the problem is compounded. He has only about
half the income of those under age 65, but—even with Medicare—he pays more than twice as much for health services.
He is doubly likely to have one or more chronic diseases than
young people, and much of the care he needs is of the most
expensive kind. And, while costs go up, services available
under Medicare and Medicaid go down—a process which
was accelerated considerably in 1971.*[10]

The committee moved on to state that in 1968 the total
benefits paid under Medicare amounted to $340 million and
in 1969 were $300 million. But in 1970 the benefits were only
$180 million, or half of what they had been.

All of these changes took place under the burden of higher
medical and surgical costs. As the committee wrote, "The
aged require twice as many doctor visits on the average and
double the amount of hospital care and prescribed drugs as
younger people so they are in 'double jeopardy' from inflation
in all these costs."

The report from the Delegates to the White House Conference on Aging asked for a coordinated delivery system for
comprehensive health services to be developed, legislated,
and financed to ensure continuity of both short- and long-
term care for the aged. They suggested that such a compre-

hensive health care plan should be legislated and financed through a National Health Plan. Until such a National Health Plan could be put into effect they required that the complete range of health care services for the elderly be provided by expanding the legislation and financing of Medicare.

Recognizing that aging begins at birth and that knowledge about it should be part of the task of every age group, these delegates also asked that emphasis be placed on including curricular or course contents on physical, mental, and social aspects of aging in secondary schools, undergraduate and graduate professional education, in in-service training, and continuing education of health personnel.

Some of the recommendations of those attending the Pre-White House Conference on Aging included increasing Social Security benefits in a manner which would give recipients of lower benefits a larger proportional lift. They talked of replacing Old Age Assistance with a new income supplement program and also suggested that an institute on retirement income be set up. The idea of establishing a special committee to devote its attention to all social and economic problems of the aged, including income, was supported also by the Delegates to the White House Conference.[11]

Inflation, unemployment, forced early retirement, poor health—all of these are demons which have removed from many older people the cloak of security and personal independence. The problem is compounded by the realization that many of the items which have risen in cost at a highly accelerated rate have been those on which older people depend. For example, medical care increased more than 30 percent from 1967 to 1971; hospital daily service charges jumped by 64 percent.[12] The older person was often likely to be the one hardest hit by the rocketing medical costs.

The statistics didn't mean much to Lily Madsen until the day she had to have delicate, and long-term, kidney surgery. Before that she had "managed" from her schoolteacher's pension, the Social Security and Medicare benefits, and the delicate kindness of her friends. Many of them had been pig-tailed children in her third-grade math class. Many of them remembered her no-nonsense teaching, iced with humor, and they brought her cakes and country eggs and took her to their homes for dinner. Miss Lily enjoyed her little apartment, sur-rounded by piles of scrapbooks and old magazines and ever-at-hand crocheting.

Illness was like a greedy hand reaching for her security. The small savings soon dissolved. When Miss Lily needed help at home after her surgery, she began to sell her family silver and the pearl-circled brooch which had been her moth-er's and her mother's before her. Miss Lily took to worrying, and her recovery slowed.

TRANSPORTATION SUGGESTIONS

Transportation and mobility are not synonymous. This point was emphasized by persons attending the Workshop on Transportation and Aging. Mobility was described as an end to be achieved and transportation as one method of reaching the desired end. In order to be mobile older people need the motivation to go from place to place, the strength to make the effort, as well as the means to reach the goal. As pointed out in the Conference, there needs to be a total mobility sys-tem enforced for older people. Widening doors to accommo-date wheelchairs will achieve no good end if the person can-not get out of his apartment or into any kind of transportation to reach the spot which has the widened doors. To help an older person reach a shopping center will be of little avail to him if he cannot negotiate his way around the center because there is no kind of transportation to take him from one place to another.

The creation of a coherent, integrated transportation serv-ice needs to be supported, according to H. W. Bruck.[13] He points out that while specialized transportation services for the elderly may be a vital interim measure, a really good sys-tem of urban transportation will serve the needs of all population groups. Mr. Bruck suggests four methods for helping the elderly in their transportation needs:

1) *improvement of access systems at both ends of the trip;*
2) *improvement in service frequency;*
3) *improvements in reliability; and*
4) *improvements in connectivity.*

In order to achieve these goals, Mr. Bruck adds, no startling new technologies are required. Instead, he feels that applying existing knowledge to the system may well help to bring about methods to make transportation accessible to many people who now are shut off from such movement.

As seen, the complexity of the transportation systems, the difficulty of reaching them, and the lack of strength for coping with many of the problems posed by present systems may seriously limit older people from making the effort to be transported anywhere for reasons of pleasure, necessity, or health.

HOUSING SUGGESTIONS

Delegates to the White House Conference on Aging recommended 25 steps which should be taken by the public and private sector in order to assure varied and adequate housing for older people. One recommendation read as follows:

A variety of living arrangements shall be made available to meet changing needs of the elderly. Such arrangements shall include residentially oriented settings for those who need different levels of assistance in daily living. The range shall include long-term care facilities for the sick; facilities with limited medical, food and homemaker services; congregate housing with food and personal services; and housing for independent living with recreational and activity programs.[14]

Other suggestions included giving special attention to the needs of all minority groups and hard-core poor elderly. The study group suggested that eligibility for benefits should be based on economic, social, and health needs. They also asked that rent supplement programs should be increased in both dollars and eligibility and that financial incentives be made available to families providing housing and related care in their own homes for their elderly relatives.

Finally, the study groups concluded with the following forceful recommendation:

Competent service to the elderly in housing requires sound research widely disseminated and utilized, covering many aspects of their living arrangements. Such research shall be undertaken to cover the health, physical, psychological, and social aspects of environment in urban and rural areas; to delineate the needs of elderly over 80 years of age; to determine the needs of transient elderly; to establish the importance of selecting appropriate locations; and to provide safe and adequate construction. Particular attention is directed to the consequences to vulnerable older people of improper sales methods and inadequate housing arrangements. There also shall be undertaken a well-conceived and well-financed program of training for professional and semi-professional staff to develop efficient and competent management in developments for the elderly.[15]

To live decently is the wish of every person. For the older person whose physical horizons may be limited and whose mobility is often impaired, good and comfortable housing becomes a necessity. Where waning energies and competencies may diminish the sense of independence, the feeling of "homeness" becomes more than a matter of comfort or location; it takes its place as a matter of self-esteem.

NUTRITION

Awareness of how serious the nutrition problem is among too many of the elderly in America was expressed by the designation of Nutrition as one of the nine "need areas" to be discussed at sections of the White House Conference on Aging. One reason for the high priority grew from the conclusions reached at the 1969 White House Conference on Nutrition. A chairman of the Panel on Aging at the Conference later said:

Selection of [nutrition and health] choices for the aged of today is a matter of national emergency requiring action of such magnitude that it can be mounted only by a dedicated Federal Government using its powers to invoke equally concerted action by State, county, and municipal authorities.[16]

In 1968 Congress earmarked two million dollars for a special program under the Administration on Aging to improve nutrition services for the elderly. The program was set up to locate people needing the program and to serve meals while building nutrition educational knowledge. It was also to provide some related services and to evaluate the work.

This government group believes that good nutrition is more than a matter of food, particularly for the older persons. In evaluating its own work the Administration on Aging stated:

Findings . . . indicate that the meal in a group setting often is the drawing card to bring lonely and isolated elderly into a whole range of the community activities. It also becomes the occasion for acquainting them with the availability of other services, or, indeed, providing such services. In such a setting, experience indicates that food-nutrition services and social-health services become mutually reinforcing in meeting the totality of the needs of the elderly participants.[17]

The demonstration programs which were implemented under the governmental aegis encompassed the multipurpose plans of seasoning food with friendship, of making concern one important ingredient of every meal. Knowing that food alone was not enough, the planners saw to it that food was only the focus around which could be built other activities—recreational, informational, counseling, and referral.

Needs of many of the elderly are complex and difficult of solution. Nevertheless, first steps have been taken in solving some of the problems raised in earlier discussion. For example, the Nutrition Program for the Elderly Act, signed on March 22, 1972, authorized $250 million over two years, starting July 1, 1972, to provide 90 percent matching money for the program. The other 10 percent is provided by state and local governments. Overall, the program is directed by the Administration on Aging through state agencies on aging where they exist.

Not only does the program become the first law to stipulate federal government funding of a nationwide program providing hot and nourishing meals to persons over 60 years of age, but it emphasizes that preference in the program be given to projects which serve low-income persons and those from minority groups.

Building on findings which have evolved from private endeavors, this public program also requires that the meals be served in convenient centers such as schools and churches and that it be within walking distance of an area where a number of the elderly live. The meals are low cost for those who can afford to pay and no cost for those who cannot.

Preference in the bill is for employment of older persons themselves wherever possible. On the other hand, it stipulates that young people should be enlisted as volunteer workers.

The bill may well provide a first and important step in reaching out in all communities to the older people who are victims of inadequate food intake and of alienation. Here companionship and good food can combine to bring older people back into the "heart of life."

What will happen to the recommendations growing out of the 1971 White House Conference depends on each of us. We are the questioners. We are also the answerers. The response will be written on the blackboard of the future.

. . . a civilization can be measured by the meaning which it gives to the full cycle of life, for such meaning, or the lack of it, cannot fail to reach into the beginnings of the next generation, and thus into the chances of others to meet ultimate questions with some clarity and strength. . . . From the stages of life, then, such dispositions as faith, will power, purposefulness, competence, fidelity, love, care, wisdom—all criteria of vital individual strength—also flow into the life of institutions. Without them, institutions wilt; but without the spirit of institutions pervading the patterns of care and love, instruction and training, no strength could emerge from the sequence of generations. Psychosocial strength, we conclude, depends on a total process which regulates individual life cycles, the sequence of generations, and the structure of society simultaneously; for all three have evolved together.[18]

·NOTES·

CHAPTER ONE

1. Erich Fromm, *Man for Himself* (New York: Rinehart and Company, 1947), p. 91.

2. Reported by Harrison J. Ullman, Associated Press, *The Louisville* (Ky.) *Courier-Journal and Times*, Sunday, April 2, 1972, p. F4.

3. Ruth Cavan, "Self and Role in Adjustment During Old Age," in *Human Behavior and Social Processes*, edited by A. M. Rose (Boston: Houghton Mifflin, 1962), pp. 527–528.

4. Paul R. Ehrlich and Anne H. Ehrlich, "The Population Crisis," in *Britannica Book of the Year* (Chicago, Toronto, London, Geneva, Sydney, Tokyo, Manila: William Benton, 1971), p. 605.

5. *Facts and Figures on Older Americans*, No. 5 (Washington, D.C.: U.S. Department of Health, Education, and Welfare, 1971), p. 2.

6. *Ibid.*, No. 21, p. 1.

7. *Statistical Abstract of the United States*, 1970 (Washington, D.C.: U.S. Department of Commerce), p. 32.

8. *Facts and Figures on Older Americans*, No. 5, p. 6.

9. *Statistical Abstract of the United States*, 1970, p. 25.

10. *Facts and Figures on Older Americans*, No. 5, p. 5.

11. *Ibid.*, p. 6.

12. *Ibid.*, pp. 7, 8.

13. *A Pre–White House Conference on Aging: Summary of Development and Data* (Washington, D.C.: U.S. Government Printing Office, 1971), p. 46.

14. *Facts and Figures*, No. 5, p. 10.

15. T. V. Smith, "On Being Retired," in *Aging in Today's Society*, edited by Clark Tibbitts and Wilma Donahue (Englewood Cliffs, N.J.: Prentice-Hall, 1960), p. 359.

16. *Ibid.*, p. 360.

17. Earl A. Grollman, *Suicide* (Boston: Beacon Press, 1971), p. 57.

18. *Ibid.*, p. 58.

19. Francis J. Braceland, M.D., "Senescence—the Inside Story," *Psychiatric Annals*, Vol. II, No. 10 (October 1972), p. 57.

20. Robert N. Butler, "Mental Health Care in Old Age: Conflicts in

Public Policy," *Psychiatric Annals*, Vol. II, No. 10 (October 1972), p. 33.

21. Wilma Donahue, "The Human Machine at Middle Life," in *Aging in Today's Society*, pp. 112–116.

22. Cited in "Sex After Forty—and After Seventy," by Isadore Rubin in *An Analysis of Human Sexual Response*, edited by Ruth and Edward Brecher (New York: The New American Library, 1966), pp. 251–252.

23. Kahlil Gibran, *The Prophet* (New York: Alfred A. Knopf, 1923), p. 90.

24. Lee Salk, "Mother's Heartbeat as an Imprinting Stimulus," in *Transactions of The New York Academy of Science*, S. 3, Vol. 24, No. 7, 1962, pp. 753–763.

25. Kahlil Gibran, *Sand and Foam* (New York: Alfred A. Knopf, 1926), p. 17.

CHAPTER TWO

1. Clark Tibbitts, "Creating a Climate for the Middle Years," in *Aging in Today's Society*, edited by Clark Tibbitts and Wilma Donahue (Englewood Cliffs, N.J.: Prentice-Hall, 1960), pp. 318–320.

2. Erich Fromm, *The Art of Loving* (New York: Bantam Books), p. 8. Originally published by Harper and Row, 1956.

3. Christine M. Morgan, "The Attitudes and Adjustments of Recipients of Old Age Assistance in Upstate and Metropolitan New York," *Archives of Psychology*, No. 214 (1937), p. 131. (*Psychological Studies of Human Development*, edited by Raymond G. Kuhlen and George C. Thompson [New York: Appleton-Century-Crofts, 1952], pp. 511–521.)

4. Rollo May, *Love and Will* (New York: W. W. Norton, 1969), p. 162.

5. Francis J. Braceland, M.D., "Senescence—the Inside Story," *Psychiatric Annals*, Vol. II, No. 10 (October 1972), p. 54.

6. Isadore Rubin, Ph.D., "Sex After Forty—and After Seventy," in *An Analysis of Human Sexual Response*, edited by Ruth and Edward Brecher (New York: The New American Library, 1966), pp. 251–266.

7. Eugene Scheimann, *Forum Magazine* (Elgin, Illinois: YMCA, April 1972).

8. Simone de Beauvoir, "Joie de Vivre," *Harper's Magazine* (January 1972), p. 34. (Originally from *The Coming of Age* [New York: G. P. Putnam's Sons, 1972].)

9. *Psychiatric News*, Vol. VII, No. 8 (April 19, 1972), p. 32.

10. Simone de Beauvoir, *loc. cit.*

11. Wilma Donahue, "The Human Machine at Middle Life," in *Aging in Today's Society*, pp. 105–116.

12. Hans Selye, "The Philosophy of Stress," in *Aging in Today's Society*, pp. 118–122.

13. *Statistical Bulletin*, Vol. 52 (New York: Metropolitan Life, September 1971), pp. 8, 9.

14. Graham Blackstock, "Aging Texans: Problems of Accidents and Health," *Texas Business Review*, Vol. XLV, No. 12 (December 1971), p. 261.

15. Edward J. Stieglitz, M.D., "The Personal Challenge of Aging: Biological Changes and Maintenance of Health," in *Aging in Today's Society*, pp. 44–53.

16. Charles M. Gaitz, M.D., and Paul E. Baer, M.D., "Diagnostic Assessment of the Elderly: A Multifunctional Model," *The Gerontologist*, Vol. 10, No. 1, Part 1 (Spring 1970), p. 47.

17. *Ibid.*, p. 48.

18. *Ibid.*, p. 49.

19. *Ibid.*, p. 47.

20. Edward M. Kennedy, *In Critical Condition: The Crisis in America's Health Care* (New York: Simon and Schuster, 1972).

21. Robert N. Butler, "Mental Health Care in Old Age: Conflicts in Public Policy," *Psychiatric Annals*, Vol. II, No. 10 (October 1972), p. 43.

22. E. G. Jaco, *The Social Epidemiology of Mental Disorders* (New York: Russell Sage Foundation, 1960), from Table 1, p. 32.

23. *Ibid.*, p. 33.

24. "Work Book on Health," Section on Health, January 1971, by White House Conference on Aging, Washington, D.C.

25. *A Report to the Delegates from the Conference Sections and Special Concerns Sessions* (Washington, D.C.: mimeographed, 1971), p. 19.

26. *A Pre–White House Conference on Aging: Summary of Development and Data* (Washington, D.C.: U.S. Government Printing Office, 1971), pp. 14, 15.

27. *Ibid.*, pp. 45, 46.

CHAPTER THREE

1. *A Pre–White House Conference on Aging: Summary of Development and Data* (Washington, D.C.: U.S. Government Printing Office, 1971).

2. *Facts and Figures on Older Americans*, No. 3 (Washington, D.C.: U.S. Department of Health, Education, and Welfare, June 1971), p. 2.

3. *A Pre–White House Conference on Aging: Development and Data*, pp. 61–63.

4. *Ibid.*, p. 60.

5. *Ibid.*, p. 61.

6. Howard P. Rome, M.D., "Introductory Remarks," *Psychiatric Annals*, Vol. II, No. 10 (October 1972), p. 10.

7. *Mental Health Care and the Elderly: Shortcomings in Public Policy* (Washington, D.C.: U.S. Government Printing Office, 1971), p. 7.

8. Robert N. Butler, M.D., "Mental Health Care in Old Age: Conflicts in Public Policy," *Psychiatric Annals*, Vol. II, No. 10 (October 1972), p. 33.

9. *The Word is Hope*, edited by Judy Bonner (Austin, Texas: The Hogg Foundation for Mental Health, 1961), pp. 18–19.

10. *Ibid.*, p. 17, 18.

11. Committee on Aging, *The Aged and Community Mental Health*, Vol. VIII, Report No. 81 (New York: Group for the Advancement of Psychiatry, November 1971), pp. 42–45.

12. *The Word is Hope*, p. 17.

13. Claire Townsend, Project Director, *Old Age: The Last Segregation*, with an Introduction by Ralph Nader (New York: Grossman Publishers, 1971), p. 20.

14. *A Pre–White House Conference on Aging: Development and Data*, p. 31.

15. "Trends in Long-Term Care," *Pre–White House Conference on Aging: Summary of Development and Data*, Part 12, pp. 1037 and 1038.

16. *Ibid.*

17. *A Pre–White House Conference on Aging: Development and Data*, p. 32.

18. Townsend, *op. cit.*, pp. 157–158.

19. *Ibid.*, p. 20. Statistics taken from *Developments in Aging, 1969: A Report of the Special Committee on Aging, U.S. Senate*, May 15, 1970, pp. 1–31.

20. Herbert Shore, "The Modern Home Responds to Change," *Professional Nursing Home* (April 1967).

21. Charles M. Gaitz, M.D., and Paul E. Baer, M.D., "Placement of Elderly Psychiatric Patients," *Journal of the American Geriatrics Society*, 1971, Vol. 19, No. 7, p. 602.

22. *Ibid.*, p. 612.

23. *Ibid.*, pp. 611–612.

24. From "Description of Some Research Findings from the Therapeutic Milieu Project," University of Michigan, Division of Gerontology, 21st Annual Conference on Aging, 1968.

25. Ormonde S. Brown, *The Work Village* (Austin, Texas: The Hogg Foundation for Mental Health, 1972).

26. Dr. Karl Menninger, "The Therapy of Friendliness," given in testimony before the Subcommittee on Long-Term Care, U.S. Senate Special Committee on Aging, hearing on "Trends in Long-Term Care," p. 5.

27. *Ibid.*; reported in *Mental Health Care and the Elderly: Shortcomings in Public Policy* (Washington, D.C.: U.S. Government Printing Office, 1971), pp. 10, 11.

28. *Mental Health Care and the Elderly: Shortcomings in Public Policy*, pp. 2–3.

29. *Ibid.*, p. 3.

30. Charles M. Gaitz, M.D., "Functional Assessment of the Suspected Mentally Ill Aged," *Journal of the American Geriatrics Society*, Vol. 17, No. 6 (June 1969), pp. 542–543.

31. Charles M. Gaitz, M.D., and Sally Hacker, "Obstacles in Coordinating Services," in *Journal of the American Geriatrics Society*, Vol. 18, No. 2 (February 1970), pp. 172–182.

32. Charles M. Gaitz, M.D., and Paul E. Baer, M.D., "Placement of Elderly Psychiatric Patients," *Journal of the American Geriatrics Society*, Vol. 19, No. 7 (July 1971), p. 601.

33. *A Report to the Delegates from the Conference Sections and Special Concerns Sessions* (Washington, D.C.: mimeographed, 1971), pp. 133–135.

34. Committee on Aging, *The Aged and Community Mental Health: A Guide to Program Development* (New York: Group for the Advancement of Psychiatry, 1971).

35. *Ibid.*, p. 15.

36. *Ibid.*, p. 33.

CHAPTER FOUR

1. Erich Fromm, *The Art of Loving* (New York: Bantam Books), p. 34. Originally published by Harper and Row, 1956.

2. Rollo May, *Love and Will* (New York: W. W. Norton, 1969), p. 284.

CHAPTER FIVE

1. Kahlil Gibran, *The Prophet* (New York: Alfred A. Knopf, 1923), p. 94.

2. Personal letter, August 28, 1972.

3. Henry A. Bowman, "The Nature of Mental Health," in *Understanding Mental Health* (Princeton: D. Van Nostrand Company, 1965); reprinted from the *General Federation Clubwoman* (October 1957), p. 39.

4. *The Word is Hope*, edited by Judy Bonner (Austin, Texas: The Hogg Foundation for Mental Health, 1961), pp. 18, 19.

5. Personal letter, August 28, 1972.

6. *The Older American* (Washington, D.C.: U.S. Government Printing Office, 1963), p. 7.

7. T. V. Smith, "On Being Retired," in *Aging in Today's Society*, edited by Clark Tibbitts and Wilma Donahue (Englewood Cliffs, N.J.: Prentice-Hall, 1960), p. 360.

8. Rueul Denny and David Riesman, "The Role of Leisure," in *ibid.*, p. 350.

9. Elisabeth Kubler-Ross, *On Death and Dying*, paperback (New York: The Macmillan Company, 1969), p. 8.

10. *Geriatric Care*, Vol. 4, No. 1 (Minneapolis: Drawer C, Ken Eymann, Editor and Publisher), p. 1.

11. *Ibid.*, p. 2.

12. *Time* Magazine, Vol. 99, No. 11, March 13, 1972 (from *New England Journal of Medicine*).

13. *Psychiatric News*, Vol. V, No. 17 (December 2, 1970), p. 19.

14. John S. Stehlin, Jr., M.D., and Kenneth H. Beach, M.D., "Psychological Aspects of Cancer Therapy," *Journal of the American Medical Association*, Vol. 197 (July 11, 1966), pp. 100–104.

15. *Ibid.*, p. 102.

16. David Hendin, NEA Science Editor, in *Austin American-Statesman* (June 1, 1972), p. B7.

17. Committee on Aging, *The Aged and Community Mental Health: A Guide to Program Development* (New York: Group for the Advancement of Psychiatry, 1971), pp. 51–52.

18. *A Report to the Delegates from the Conference Sections and Special Concerns Sessions* (Washington, D.C.: mimeographed, 1971), p. 38.

CHAPTER SIX

1. *A Pre–White House Conference on Aging: Summary of Development and Data* (Washington, D.C.: U.S. Government Printing Office, 1971), p. 102.

2. John B. Martin, Commissioner of the Administration on Aging, *Let's End Isolation*, Foreword to Administration of Aging Publication No. 121 (Washington, D.C.: U.S. Government Printing Office, June 1971).

3. *Food Consumption and Dietary Levels of Older Households in Rochester, New York* (Washington, D.C.: U.S. Department of Agriculture, 1965).

4. *Activity Report* (Denton, Texas: Denton State School, November 30, 1971 [mimeographed]), p. 10.

5. *Ibid.*, p. 13.

6. *Program Information Statement, RSVP* (Washington, D.C.: ACTION, January 1972).

7. *The Older Volunteer Speaks on New Roles in Retirement* (New

York: Department of Public Affairs, Committee on Aging, 105 E. 22nd Street [mimeographed]), p. 48.

8. *The Golden Years: A Tarnished Myth* (Washington, D.C.: The National Council on Aging, Inc., January 16, 1972, reprinted March 1972 [mimeographed]), p. 4.

9. Betty Murphy, "Finding the 'Invisible' Elderly Poor," *Opportunity*, Vol. 1, No. 8 (Washington, D.C.: Office of Public Affairs, November 1971), p. 2.

10. *Ibid.*

11. *The Nation's Stake in the Employment of Middle-Aged and Older Persons* (Washington, D.C.: U.S. Government Printing Office, 1971), p. 33.

12. *Ibid.*, p. 35.

13. *Ibid.*, pp. 43–45.

14. Eleanor Gurewitsch, Christian Science Monitor News Service, in *Austin American-Statesman* (May 18, 1972), p. B16.

15. John H. Bell, "Senior Citizens Mobile Service," in *Transportation and Aging*, edited by Edmund J. Cantilli and June L. Shmelzer (Washington, D.C.: U.S. Government Printing Office, 1970), pp. 138–139.

16. Harold L. Willson, "The Elderly and Handicapped on the San Francisco Bay Area Transit System," in *ibid.*, pp. 159–161.

17. *Ibid.*, p. 18.

18. Louis J. Pignataro, Introduction to *ibid.*, p. 6.

CHAPTER SEVEN

1. Erik H. Erikson, *Identity: Youth and Crisis* (New York: W. W. Norton, 1968), p. 139.

2. *Ibid.*, p. 140.

3. *A New Concept of Aging* (Chicago: American Medical Association, 1963), p. 6.

4. *Mental Health Care and the Elderly: Shortcomings in Public Policy* (Washington, D.C.: U.S. Government Printing Office, 1971), p. 147.

5. *Ibid.*, pp. 149, 150.

6. Gerald Caplan, *Principles of Preventive Psychiatry* (New York: Basic Books, 1964), p. 61.

7. *Ibid.*, p. 62.

8. Erikson, *op. cit.*, p. 141.

9. Kahlil Gibran, *The Prophet* (New York: Alfred A. Knopf, 1931), pp. 70–71.

APPENDIX

1. *Mental Health Care and the Elderly: Shortcomings in Public Policy* (Washington, D.C.: U.S. Government Printing Office, 1971), p. 29.

2. *Ibid.*, pp. 30, 31.

3. From *SOS.5* (Washington, D.C.: The National Council on Aging, 1970 [duplicated]), p. 4.

4. *Senior Opportunities and Services Technical Assistance Monograph* (Washington, D.C.: The National Council on Aging, 1970), p. 5.

5. Proposals for a National Policy on Aging (Washington, D.C.: National Retired Teachers Association and the American Association of Retired Persons, 1971 [duplicated]), p. 2.

6. *Ibid.*, p. 3.

7. *A Report to the Delegates from the Conference Sections and Special Concerns Sessions* (Washington, D.C.: mimeographed, 1971), pp. 66, 67.

8. *Ibid.*, p. 66.

9. *Ibid.*, pp. 68, 69.

10. *A Pre–White House Conference on Aging: Summary of Development and Data* (Washington, D.C.: U.S. Government Printing Office, 1971), p. 17.

11. *A Report to the Delegates from the Conference Sections and Special Concerns Sessions*, pp. 19, 22.

12. *Ibid.*, pp. 8, 14, 15.

13. H. W. Bruck, "Emerging and Novel Transportation Systems as They Apply to the Elderly," in *Transportation and Aging, Selected Issues*, edited by Edmund J. Cantilli and June L. Shmelzer (Washington, D.C.: U.S. Government Printing Office, 1970), pp. 107–113.

14. *A Report to the Delegates from the Conference Sections and Special Concerns Sessions*, p. 16.

15. *Ibid.*, p. 18.

16. *A Pre–White House Conference on Aging: Summary of Development and Data* (from a statement by Donald M. Watkin, at the First Annual Joseph A. Desprs Conference for Senior Citizens, New York Ciity, January 22, 1971), p. 98.

17. *A Pre–White House Conference on Aging: Summary of Development and Data*, p. 98.

18. Erik H. Erikson, *Identity: Youth and Crisis* (New York: W. W. Norton, 1968), pp. 140, 141.

Information on Aging

RESOURCES

(Clearinghouse)
National Center for Voluntary
  Action
Paramount Building
1735 Eye Street, N.W.
Washington, D.C.   20006

National Council on the Aging
1828 L Street, N.W., Suite 502
Washington, D.C.   20036

Works with and through other organizations:
  —provides a national information and consultation center
  —holds workshops
  —sponsors awards

Administration on Aging
Dr. Walter Moeller
HEW South Building, Rm. 3609
Third and C Streets, S.W.
Washington, D.C.   20201

Provides counsel, advice, and guidance to any voluntary group interested in working with and for the aging; publishes a free manual for "Concerns for the Elderly" overall project.

Retired Senior Volunteer Program
ACTION
806 Connecticut Avenue, N.W.
Washington, D.C.   20525

Provides grants for the development and operation of programs providing community volunteer opportunities for persons 60 years of age and over. Information available from appropriate State Offices on Aging as well as national office.

National Retired Teachers Association

American Association of Retired Persons

1225 Connecticut Avenue, N.W.

Washington, D.C.   20036

Administers programs for the aged; operates volunteer programs on a community level; sponsors workshops; publishes a variety of guide booklets on retirement and a bimonthly magazine, *Modern Maturity*.

DIRECTORIES

Directory of National Organizations with Programs in the Field of Aging
Prepared by the Office of Economic Opportunity
by the National Council on Aging
1828 L Street, N.W.
Washington, D.C.   20036

DIRECTORY OF STATE AGENCIES DESIGNATED TO ADMINISTER TITLE III OF THE OLDER AMERICANS ACT

Symbols
° Agency designated to implement Older Americans Program
Unit responsible for day-to-day operations of the Older Americans Program

ALABAMA

° # Commission on Aging
740 Madison Avenue
Montgomery   36104

ALASKA

° Department of Health &
Social Services,
Pouch H
Juneau   99801

Office of Aging
Department of Health &
Social Services,
Pouch H
Juneau   99801

ARIZONA

° Department of Public
Welfare, State Office
Building
1624 West Adams Street
Phoenix   85007

Division for Aging
State Department of Public
Welfare
1624 West Adams Street
Phoenix   85007

ARKANSAS

° Dept. of Social & Rehabilitation Services
601-3 Capitol Hill Bldg.
Little Rock   72201

Office on Aging
4313 W. Markham, Hendrix
Hall
P.O. Box 2179
Little Rock   72203

CALIFORNIA

° Department of Human Re-
sources Development—
Office Bldg. #1
915 Capitol Mall
Sacramento   95814

✳ Commission on Aging
800 Capitol Mall, Rm. 2105
Sacramento   95814

COLORADO

✱ Department of Social Services
1575 Sherman Street
Denver   80203

✳ Division of Services for the Aging
Department of Social Services
1575 Sherman Street
Denver   80203

CONNECTICUT

✱ ✳ Department on Aging
90 Washington Street
Room 312
Hartford   06115

DELAWARE

✱ Department of Health & Social Services
P.O. Box 309
Wilmington   19805

✳ Bureau of Aging
Division of Social Services
2407 Lancaster Ave.
Wilmington   19805

DISTRICT OF COLUMBIA

✱ ✳ Department of Human Resources
122 C Street, N.W.
Room 803
Washington   20001

✱ ✳ Office of Services to the Aged
Dept. of Human Resources
122 C Street, N.W.
Washington   20001

FLORIDA

✱ Department of Health & Rehabilitative Services
IBM Branch Office Building
660 Appalachia Parkway
Tallahassee   32304

✳ Division of Family Services
Department of Health & Rehabilitative Services
P.O. Box 2050
Jacksonville   32203

GEORGIA

✱ ✳ Georgia Dept. of Human Resources
Office of Aging
1372 Peachtree Street, N.E.
Atlanta   30309

GUAM

✱ Dept. of Public Health & Social Services
P.O. Box 2816
Agana   96813

✳ Office of Aging
Dept. of Public Health & Social Services
P.O. Box 2816
Agana   96813

HAWAII

✱ ✳ Commission on Aging
250 S. King Street
Honolulu   96813

IDAHO

° Department of Special Services
Capitol Annex #7
509 North 5th Street
Boise   83707

‡ Office on Aging
Capitol Annex #7
509 North 5th Street
Boise   83707

ILLINOIS

° Department of Public Aid
State Office Building
618 E. Washington St.
Springfield   62706

‡ Section on Services for Aging
Illinois Dept. of Public Aid
209 W. Jackson Blvd., Rm. 602
Chicago, Illinois   60606

INDIANA

° ‡ Indiana Commission on the Aging and Aged
Graphic Arts Bldg.
215 North Senate Ave.
Indianapolis   46202

IOWA

° ‡ Commission on Aging
415 10th Street
Des Moines, Iowa   50319

KANSAS

° Department of Social Welfare
State Office Bldg.
Topeka   66612

‡ Division of Services for the Aging
Department of Social Welfare
State Office Bldg.
Topeka   66612

KENTUCKY

° ‡ Commission on Aging
Capitol Plaza Office Tower, 8th Floor
Frankfort   40601

LOUISIANA

° ‡ Commission on Aging
P.O. Box 44282
Capitol Station
Baton Rouge   70804

MAINE

° Department of Health & Welfare
State House
Augusta   04330

‡ Services for Aging
Community Services Unit
Department of Health & Welfare
State House
Augusta   04330

MARYLAND

° Dept. of Employment Security and Social Services
Rm. 600
1100 North Eutaw Street
Baltimore   21201

‡ Commission on Aging
State Office Bldg.
301 West Preston Street
Baltimore   21201

MASSACHUSETTS

° Dept. of Elder Affairs
State Office Building
18 Tremont St.
Boston   02109

≠ Bureau of Aging
Dept. of Elder Affairs
141 Milk Street
Boston   02109

MICHIGAN

° ≠ Commission on Aging
Dept. of Social Services
Commerce Center Building
300 South Capitol Ave.
Lansing   48926

MINNESOTA

° # Governor's Citizen's Council on Aging
277 West University Ave.
St. Paul   55103

MISSISSIPPI

° ≠ Council on Aging
P.O. Box 5136, Fondren Station
2906 North State Street
Jackson   39216

MISSOURI

° Dept. of Community Affairs
505 Missouri Blvd.
Jefferson City   65101

≠ Office of Aging
Dept. of Community Affairs
505 Missouri Blvd.
Jefferson City   65101

MONTANA

° ≠ Commission on Aging
Penkay Eagles Manor
715 Fee Street
Helena   59601

NEBRASKA

° ≠ Commission on Aging
State House Station 94784
Lincoln   68509

NEVADA

° Dept. of Health, Welfare
and Rehabilitation
515 East Musser Street
Carson City   89701

≠ Division of Aging Services
Dept. of Health, Welfare
and Rehabilitation
308 North Curry Street
Carson City   89701

NEW HAMPSHIRE

° ≠ Council on Aging
P.O. Box 786
71 South Main St.
Concord   03301

NEW JERSEY

° ≠ Division on Aging
Dept. of Community Affairs
P.O. Box 2768
363 West State Street
Trenton   08625

NEW MEXICO

° ≠ State Commission on Aging
408 Galisteo—Villagra Bldg.
Santa Fe   87501

NEW YORK

° ‡ Office for the Aging
N.Y. State Exec. Dept.
855 Central Avenue
Albany   12206

NORTH CAROLINA

° ‡ Governor's Coordinating
Council on Aging
213 Hillsborough Street
Raleigh   27603

NORTH DAKOTA

° Public Welfare Board
State Capitol Building
Bismark   58501

‡ Programs on Aging
Public Welfare Board
Randal Professional Bldg.
Route I
Bismark   58501

OHIO

° Department of Mental Hy-
giene and Correction
State Office Building
Columbus   43215

‡ Division of Administration
on Aging
Department of Mental Hy-
giene and Correction
State Office Building
Columbus   43215

OKLAHOMA

° Dept. of Institutions
Social & Rehabilitative
Services
Box 25352, Capitol Station
Oklahoma City   73125

‡ Special Unit on Aging
Dept. of Institutions
Social & Rehabilitative
Services
Box 25352, Capitol Station
Oklahoma City   73125

OREGON

° Human Resources Dept.
318 Public Service Building
Salem   97310

‡ State Program on Aging
318 Public Service Building
Salem   97310

PENNSYLVANIA

° Department of Public Wel-
fare
Health & Welfare Building
Harrisburg   17120

‡ Bureau for the Aging
Office of Adult Programs
Department of Public Wel-
fare
Harrisburg   17120

PUERTO RICO

° Department of Social Serv-
ices
P.O. Box 11697
Santurce   00908

‡ Gericulture Commission
Dept. of Social Services
P.O. Box 11697
Santurce   00908

RHODE ISLAND

° Dept. of Community Affairs
289 Promenade Street
Providence   02903

\# Division of Services for
    Aging
Department of Community
    Affairs
289 Promenade Street
Providence   02903

\## SAMOA

* * Dept. of Manpower Re-
    sources
Pago Pago, American Samoa
    96920

\## SOUTH CAROLINA

* \# Commission on Aging
2414 Bull Street
Columbia   29201

\## SOUTH DAKOTA

* State Department of Health
Pierre   57501

\# Programs on Aging
State Department of Health
Pierre   57501

\## TENNESSEE

* \# Commission on Aging
510 Gay Street
Capitol Towers
Nashville   37219

\## TEXAS

* \# Governor's Committee on
    Aging
P.O. Box 12786
Capitol Station
Austin   78711

\## TRUST TERRITORY of
    the PACIFIC

* \# Office of Aging
Government of the Trust

Territory of the Pacific
    Islands
Saipan, Mariana Islands
    96950

\## UTAH

* Dept. of Social Services
221 State Capitol Building
Salt Lake City   84114

\# Division of Aging
345 South Sixth Street
Salt Lake City   84102

\## VERMONT

* \# Interdepartmental Council
    on Aging
126 Main Street
Montpelier   05602

\## VIRGINIA

* Division of State Planning &
    Community Affairs
109 Governor Street
Richmond   23219

\# Gerontology Planning Sec-
    tion
Div. of State Planning &
    Community Affairs
109 Governor Street
Richmond   23219

\## VIRGIN ISLANDS

* \# Virgin Island Commission
    on Aging
P.O. Box 539
Charlotte Amalie
St. Thomas   00801

\## WASHINGTON

* Department of Social &
    Health Services

P.O. Box 1788
Olympia   98504

⧣ State Unit on Aging
   Dept. of Social & Health
        Services
   P.O. Box 1162
   Olympia   98501

   WEST VIRGINIA

❋ ⧣ Commission on Aging
      State Capitol, Rm. 420–26
      1800 Wash. St. East
      Charleston   25305

   WISCONSIN

❋ Dept. of Health & Social
        Services
   State Office Bldg., Rm. 690
   1 West Wilson Street
   Madison   53702

⧣ Division on Aging
   Dept. of Health & Social
        Services
   State Office Bldg., Rm. 690
   1 West Wilson Street
   Madison   53702

   WYOMING

❋ Dept. of Health & Social
        Services
   State Office Building
   Cheyenne   82001

⧣ Aging Services
   Dept. of Health & Social
        Services
   State Office Building
   Cheyenne   82001

PUBLICATIONS

National Council on Aging
Publications List
1828 L Street, N.W.
Washington, D.C.   20036

INDEX